Underground
Movement

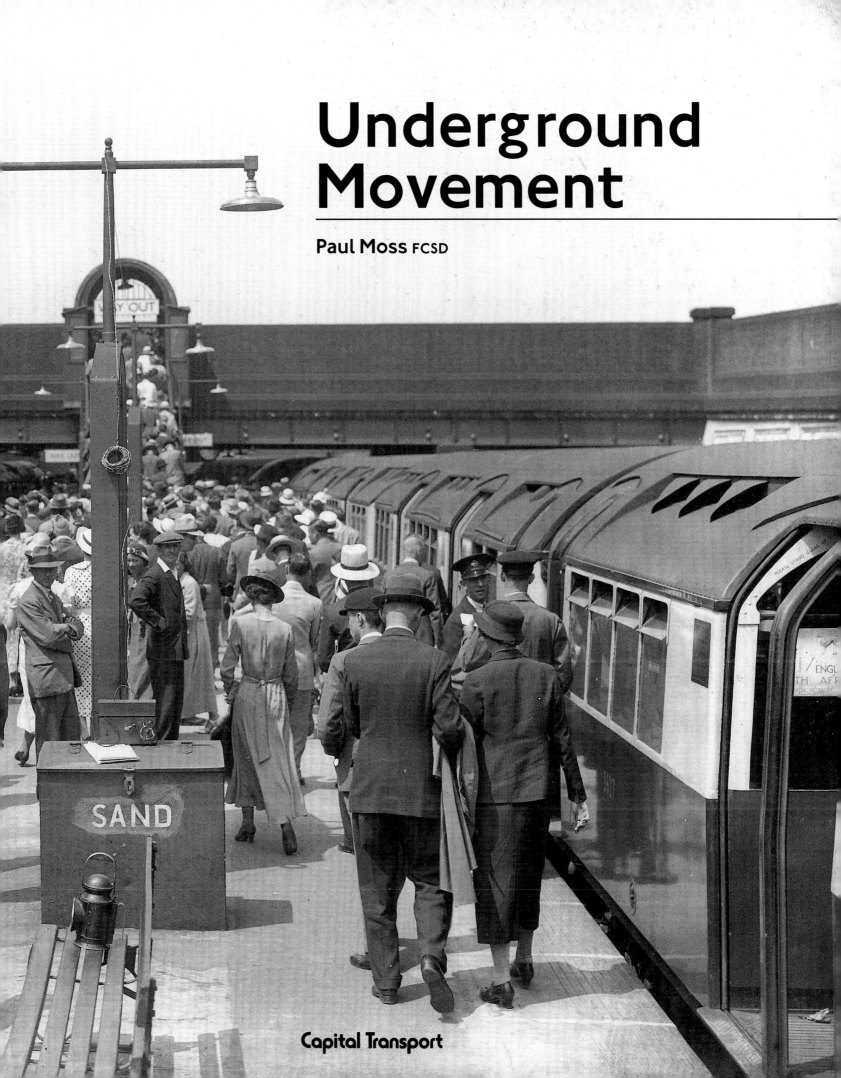

Underground Movement

Paul Moss FCSD

Capital Transport

Author's Note

ISBN 1 85414 226 7

Published by Capital Transport Publishing
38 Long Elmes, Harrow Weald, Middlesex

Printed by CS Graphics, Singapore

Designed by Tim Demuth

ACKNOWLEDGEMENTS

I would like to thank the following individuals and
organisations for their valued time and enthusiastic help
and support given to me while researching this book:

The late Bob Greenaway, London Underground, and
Oliver Green, who both proof-read the initial text

Brian Hardy and Mike Horne, who checked the final
draft

David Carter, Michael Groves and Paul Rutter, DCA
Design Consultants

Martin Pemberton, Warwick Design Consultants

Maurice Green and Jim Williams, Design Research Unit

From London Underground:
    Malcolm Dobell, Chris Sharp and Andrew Dean, for
    their much appreciated help and enthusiasm in
    providing information and material for the final
    'Space train' and 'Accessible train' chapter;
    Philip Shrapnell, for his help in providing information
    and material for the New Jubilee and Northern Line
    trains chapter;
    Warren Kencroft, for his help in providing
    information on the D stock refurbishment

Sheila Taylor, London's Transport Museum

David Hallgarth and Rodney Hirst, John Holdsworth
& Co. Ltd, who not only carefully researched the design
background of eight of the most significant historical
moquette patterns but also generously had them
woven especially for reproduction in this book

Trevor Scott, Trevor Scott Associates

Richard Seymour and Dick Powell, Seymour-Powell
Design

Marvin Shane, Tilney Shane

Siep Wijsenbeek, Design Triangle

Chris Ludlow, Henrion Ludlow and Schmidt

Haydon Williams, Haydon Williams International

Over the years there has been an abundance of books and publications written about London Underground's trains, but for the most part these have tended to concentrate on the technical development of the rolling stock and associated operational factors. Their unique and fascinating carbody design history has not before been covered. This is surprising because the images of these trains are powerful ones and they have been intrinsically woven into the fabric of London's continuing development and social history over the last 100 years. The often subliminal design statements that they make or have made are received by millions of travellers every day and there is not doubt that many are compelling ones. The moquette patterns designed in the pre- and just post-war periods still hold a tremendous nostalgic appeal for those Londoners who can recall them, as does the memory of the warm, inviting and supremely comfortable interiors of the classic 1938 tube stock.

This book documents and celebrates the tremendous achievements of the many talented people from both inside and outside the Underground who have shaped over the last eighty years the trains that Londoners and visitors to the capital have used. Also, unfulfilled concepts are described and illustrated, many of them published for the first time. During the seven and a half years that I spent as London Underground's Design Manager, I was privileged to work closely with all of the British Industrial Design consultancies involved on the refurbishment and new built rolling stock projects that are described in the book. It is appropriate to record the significant contribution and added value that these design companies, working closely with the Underground's own engineers, client teams and contractors have made to all of the train types currently in service. Historical advice has been given during this book's preparation by Mike Horne and Brian Hardy. I am very grateful to them both for their corrections to the draft.

Finally, I would like to dedicate this book to two people. One is my late father, Joseph Moss, who unwittingly instilled in me at five years old, a certain abiding interest in London's Underground trains! All the time my mother and I were living in Ashton-under-Lyne in Lancashire and he was working in London and looking for a place to live. I vividly remember a letter that he sent in which, for my benefit, he had sketched some drawings of what tube trains looked like, complete with 'LONDON TRANSPORT' on the side. I could not wait to come down and see them, such are the powerful influences that can affect us in our early days!

The other is Bob Greenaway who was a walking encyclopedia on absolutely anything to do with Underground trains and their history. Bob was very enthusiastic about this book and helped me enormously during its preparation. Working with him was a constant pleasure due to not only his detailed and erudite knowledge and also his friendly encouragement at all times. He joined London Transport at the age of 20 as an engineer and after working with London Underground for 35 years, died suddenly in the middle of last year. His pleasant, easy manner is greatly missed by all who knew him.

Bookham, Surrey, September 2000   PAUL MOSS

Contents

CHAPTER ONE

Introduction

A portrait of Frank Pick taken during his early years with the Underground Electric Railways Company of London Ltd (UERL).

Below One of the multiple-unit electric trains which replaced the locomotives on the Central London Railway in 1903. In design terms, the cab and control equipment section was simply grafted onto the existing trailer car and they sat on top of a raised section which cleared the power bogie. This layout would be followed for all Underground tube stock motor cars for the next thirty years. By good fortune this important historical link exists today in a surviving sleet locomotive at London's Transport Museum's Depot at Acton. This loco was converted in 1939 from two ex Central London Railway driving motor cars following their removal from passenger service. The cab design with its uniquely faceted roof makes a fascinating contrast with those of the latest Underground trains.

This book traces the design development of London's Underground trains from the early 1920s to the end of the 20th Century and also takes a glimpse into the future to see what tomorrow's ideas and technologies might bring. It was in the 1920s that the Underground began to develop a style of its own in train design. Frank Pick, who was later to play such a pivotal role in the realisation of London Transport's internationally acclaimed design excellence, had been made Assistant Managing Director of its predecessor organisation, the Underground Group, in 1921. We will see in the second chapter how he very soon started to shape and influence the external manifestation of that Group's business activities.

However, in order to put all of Pick's work fully into perspective, it is important to understand and briefly trace the history behind all that he inherited in the post First World War period. In particular, the remarkable American influence that had shaped London's underground railways since the early 1900s.

During the the latter half of the 19th century there had been massive investment in the building of steam hauled underground railways, the finance for which had come from private sources. The new steam underground railways in London used 'cut and cover' railway building technology and the tracks created formed the nucleus of a rail transport network which remains with us today, for parts of the Metropolitan, District, Hammersmtih & City and Circle lines run on these same routes. The trains that operate on these particular lines are of similar size to main-line trains and are called surface stock.

'Cut and cover' construction was eventually to be used to create the below-street urban railways of other European capital cities such as Budapest, Berlin, Paris and Vienna but nowhere else in the world is there also to be found the extensive system of bored circular tunnels which characterise the construction of London's deep level

underground lines. The capital's 'blue' clay is an ideal medium through which to tunnel and this fact led to a large and rapid extension of various lines under the city during the Edwardian period. Designing and building trains that can comfortably carry huge numbers of passengers safely and speedily through these circular tube tunnels remains to this day a challenge which, apart from the small tube system in Glasgow, is not faced by any other operator of Metro trains in the world.

The first line to run in twin circular bored tube tunnels was the City & South London Railway which was opened at the end of 1890. With rolling stock hauled by electric locomotives, it originally ran from Stockwell to King William Street in the City of London with four intermediate stations (Oval, Kennington, Elephant & Castle, Borough). Subsequent lines were: The Waterloo & City Railway (opened in 1898), The Central London Railway from Shepherd's Bush to Bank (1900), The Baker Street & Waterloo Railway from Elephant & Castle to Baker Street (1906), The Great Northern, Piccadilly & Brompton Railway from Finsbury Park to Hammersmith (1906) and The Charing Cross, Euston & Hampstead Railway (1907).

The Central London Railway certainly promised the best financial return for it was planned to run underneath one of London's busiest bus routes from the Bank of England via Cheapside, Holborn, Oxford Street, Bayswater Road through to Shepherd's Bush. It opened in the middle of 1900 and unlike the City & South London,

Above left The interior of one of the first Central London Railway cars of 1900. Note the formed perforated wooden seating, the turned seat legs with matching armrest infills, the luggage racks and the elegant *art nouveau* style lampshades incorporating an intertwined CLR symbol. By 1903 the seats had already been upholstered with a more comfortable sprung rattan weave (or split cane) material. Handgrips and small racks for items such as hats, umbrellas and small parcels were fitted from the outset.

Above right By 1908 the lampshades had been replaced by more perfunctory shaded lamps and route maps had appeared on the ceiling.

A second line of design development has been that of the trains for the 'surface stock' lines. This is a 1905 District Railway surface stock motor car built in Britain under the influence of a design team from America.

Charing Cross, Euston & Hampstead motor car and trailer of 1907 showing the lattice gates at the ends of cars.

was of sufficient size and power to be a financial success; the diameter of its tunnels being 16 inches bigger allowed larger rolling stock to be used. Mark Twain, the great American author, was present at the opening and his presence foreshadowed an increasingly powerful American interest in the destinies and fortunes of London's new urban railways. At its outset, the cars on the 'Twopenny Tube' (as it was called because of its flat rate fare) were hauled by heavy 44 ton 'camel-backed' American built electric locomotives, but the considerable noise and vibration which they produced caused serious annoyance to the residents who lived above the line. The line had to do something quickly to remain in business and so in 1901 four of the wooden passenger cars were converted into motor cars to test the then newly invented Sprague-Thomson-Houston multiple-unit control system. This system had been invented by Frank Julian Sprague, an American inventor and entrepreneur and had been first introduced in Chicago in 1898. Motors and control equipment could be fitted to some or all of the passenger cars forming a train, linked by low-voltage control circuits, thus allowing operation from one controller in the cab of the leading car. These prototypes were resoundingly successful, proving the vastly superior performance of multiple-unit trains, not only from the viewpoint of greatly reduced vibration but also allowing much greater flexibility at termini, since with a cab fitted at both ends, trains could now be driven in either direction without turning the whole train (via a loop) or running the loco round the train.

Orders were therefore placed for 64 new motor cars and these were delivered in 1903. When formed into trains with existing trailer cars, these and the prototypes already mentioned were not only the first multiple-unit trains to be placed in passenger service in Britain but also the true progenitors of all subsequent tube train designs. As originally built, their wooden bodies featured an external livery of white and purplish brown with the title CENTRAL LONDON in four inch high gold letters. The original interiors of the 1900 cars featured padded armrests and formed and perforated wood panelled seating, but by 1903 this had already been re-upholstered with a more comfortable sprung rattan weave material.

The financial success of the Central London Railway led to a flood of bills in the 1901 parliamentary session but by then there had appeared on the scene an American with a uniquely extensive knowledge of urban transport electrification and its financing. This was the colourful and ostentatious Charles Tyson Yerkes who had made a fortune from Chicago's rapid transit system. In the familiar manner of how the workings of that city have always operated, this had involved making extensive bribes to all of the leading city dignitaries! However, in England, his financial advisor was Edgar Speyer, a more sober influence who was head of a London merchant bank with offices in New York and Frankfurt.

The first scarlet and cream Baker Street & Waterloo Railway driving motor car, built by the American Car & Foundry Company and then finally assembled at their Trafford Park works in Manchester. It is seen new in 1906.

Yerkes had considerable practical experience of lucrative tramway and local railway promotions in the States and therefore found the new underground railway lines that had been sanctioned by Parliament, awaiting finance, to be irresistible!

In 1901 he not only had already secured effective control of the District Railway which was now ripe for electrification, but also had acquired most of the companies who had already obtained the parliamentary powers to build deep level tube railways. These were brought together in 1902 under the name of the Underground Electric Railways Company of London Limited (the Underground Group.) The three UERL tubes were built at a fast pace, all of them being open for business by the end of 1907. Most of the tube stations in the central London area that now carry millions of commuters each week are the result of that heady period of activity.

To give some idea of the work pressures involved, more than 40 of these stations were opened on the three Underground Group tube lines between 1906 and 1907. Leslie Green, the architect who designed all of them with their familiar ox-blood glazed external faience brickwork died the following year at the tragically early age of 33 from tuberculosis, which was possibly hastened as a result of the tremendously demanding work loads imposed by the Yerkes regime.

The management of the District Railway brought over a team of engineers from America and electric trains were already in operation between South Acton and South Harrow by 1903. Predictably these were totally American in style with clerestory roofs, vertical wood planked bodies, arched windows and open gated ends. The seating was finished in rattan and the earliest cars were painted in bright yellow, picked out in maroon, but later builds had an all over maroon colour scheme with the doors left in their natural varnished wood finish. They were built in Britain and France.

The trains for the Yerkes tube lines were essentially of a common design and were ordered in quantity from French, Hungarian and American manufacturers, although the latter vehicles were assembled in England. The reason given for procuring all of these vehicles from outside the UK was that British manufacturers had little experience at the time of building the all steel bodywork which was a basic safety requirement for the new tube stock. The Board of Trade was now insisting on this form of construction because of the greatly improved fire safety performance ratings which could be achieved. In addition it was stated that the delivery lead times that were being offered by these foreign manufacturers were much shorter than what the equivalent UK companies could achieve, but in reality most of the British concerns had never even been asked to tender! These cars, like those on the CLR, all featured gated ends. This operating practice was not ideal because access to and from the saloon areas could be slow and congested and furthermore, each pair of adjacent gates required its own gateman.

Albert Stanley in 1910.

Cars on the Baker Street & Waterloo Railway were painted in a very smart livery of cream and scarlet, but the Great Northern, Piccadilly & Brompton Railway cars were, like the District line's vehicles, painted in a deep maroon with the centre cab door left in natural varnished wood finish. Interiors were similarly fitted out with rattan seating.

Unfortunately for the UERL's shareholders, traffic was still not reaching Yerkes' optimistic forecasts, but by that time he personally was no longer part of the action, having died in New York at the end of 1905. The American shareholders sent over their own trouble-shooter to sort things out and they appointed him as general manager at the then remarkably generous salary of £2,000 a year. He was a 32 year old tramway expert, born in England, but who had spent most of his life in America. He had risen from working as an odd job man on the Detroit tramways and his name was Albert Stanley. Later on in 1920 he became Lord Ashfield and although he initially came on just a three year contract, he was to dominate London's transport scene for the next 40 years.

He joined George Stegmann Gibb who had been 'head-hunted' as managing director from the North Eastern Railway by Yerkes' successor as chairman, Edgar Speyer. Gibb took up office on January 1st 1906 and had brought down with him from York a younger colleague, a certain Frank Pick who, with a London law degree, had already shown great promise in pioneering modern management methods on the North Eastern Railway.

This new team saved the UERL from financial disaster, for the working losses turned to gains in 1908. Gibb left in 1910 and Albert Stanley succeeded him as managing director at the age of 37. They then went forward to acquire the London General Omnibus Company, the Central London Railway, the City & South London Railway, the Metropolitan Electric Tramways and consolidated the operation of the other major tramway company under their control – London United Tramways, which had already been purchased by Yerkes. Albert Stanley was knighted in 1914 in recognition of his services to London's transport and the scene was now set for the significant years which still lay ahead.

This photograph clearly shows the inherent problems caused by the layout of the gate stock cars. One of the team of gatemen can be seen standing between the gated ends of two Yerkes vehicles at Elephant & Castle station in 1924. They had to supervise loading and unloading, ensuring that everyone was safely on board before manually closing the gates. Surprisingly these problems were nevertheless effectively overcome because even prior to 1920 train frequencies of over 40 trains an hour were quite possible! It was not until 1929 that the very last gate stock cars on the system were finally withdrawn from the Bakerloo Line.

Finally, in this introduction, a look at two further tube vehicle types that date from the period before the First World War which created the transitional step between the pre- and post-war designs.

In 1914 new all-steel motor cars were bought from the Leeds Forge Company and Brush of Loughborough for the Bakerloo Line extensions to Queen Park and Willesden Junction. These were the first tube cars to be built with middle doors, albeit still manually operated. Twenty-four similar motor cars were ordered in 1912 for the Central London Railway's planned extension out to Ealing Broadway. They were also provided with central swing doors but for the first time these were used with enclosed car ends. Heaters were also fitted which was a response to the fact that tube trains now had to operate in the open air as well.

Twelve six-car trains were ordered from The Metropolitan Carriage, Wagon and Finance Co., also with enclosed ends, for the service from the Bakerloo tunnels out to Watford using the tracks of the London & North Western Railway. Known as the LER-LNWR Joint Stock with a one third/two thirds ownership split, their floors were 4½ inches higher than that of the original tube stock, the level being a compromise between the heights of the tube and the LNWR suburban platforms. Their operational performance was soon to be outclassed by the later introduction of Standard Stock and they were all scrapped a mere eleven years later.

Above One of the driving motor cars built by Leeds Forge in 1914 for the Bakerloo extensions, still with end gates fitted. These were, however, the first production tube cars to be fitted with middle doors, although not as yet air-operated.

A trailer car interior of the Bakerloo LNWR joint stock: 32 out of a total of 48 moquette covered seats were arranged transversely; this was made possible because the higher floor level cleared the wheels.

Left One of the Brush built motor cars that were ordered in 1912 for the extension to Ealing Broadway and delivered in 1917. This was the first tube stock design whose fully enclosed doors finally eliminated the gated ends. Thus it is the final link with the first air operated tube stock described in the next chapter.

CHAPTER TWO

The years 1920 to 1933

TUBE STOCK TRAINS

The early post First World War years were particularly significant for a number of reasons. First of all, the very first tube stock to be designed with air operated automatic doors (1920 Tube Stock) was ordered from Cammell Laird in 1919 for the Piccadilly Line (these were later transferred to the Bakerloo around 1930). Forty cars were delivered (20 control trailers, i.e. with cabs but no traction equipment and 20 trailers). They were delivered at the end of 1920 but could not be used in passenger service until 20 ex-Piccadilly Line, 1906 Hungarian-built gate stock motor cars had been converted to run with them. The end gates of these were filled in, replaced by powered end doors and the centre of each car was altered to accommodate air operated double doors. Thus a major technical and operational breakthrough was achieved where for the first time, the number of gatemen per train could be reduced from one serving two car ends, which the gate stock demanded, to two guards per train. (On these trains the two guards were placed in the trailing ends of the two motor cars included in a 6-car set.)

The exterior design of the control trailers featured elliptical cab windows (unique on any tube stock) and retained the characteristic bulging body section of the old Yerkes type 1906 gate stock cars. The doors, however, did not follow this profile – they

Top This photograph of 1920 Stock entering Charing Cross station clearly shows how its elliptical cab windows hindered the driver's visibility. No destination display has been fitted!

Right The interior of a Cammell Laird trailer car as originally built for the Piccadilly Line in 1922, with leather type upholstery, no arm rests and cement flooring. Note the shortened seats with their almost upright backs fitted against the door pockets, which must have been extremely uncomfortable! Seventy years would elapse before continuous horizontal handrails over longitudinal seats would make their next appearance in tube trains.

were essentially flat and were only shaped at the top to follow the curvature of the roof. The double doors closed against a massive central pillar which had a pilot lamp fitted on it. When illuminated, this indicated to the guard that these doors were not fully closed. Instead of individual strap hangers, the interior of these cars featured continuous horizontal handrails, a feature that would reappear seventy years later on refurbished and new trains! Longitudinal seats were fitted throughout, upholstered in a synthetic leather material and no armrests were fitted. These were the last trains to be ordered, designed and built in an ad-hoc manner for the Underground Group.

Frank Pick, who had been made Joint Assistant Managing Director of the Underground Group in 1921, under the chairmanship of Lord Ashfield, knew that for the future, there had to be better solutions to meet the business requirements and objectives of the organisation. His lifelong crusade was to present the London Underground system as a bold, dynamic forward looking enterprise where its every manifestation would announce it to both passengers and staff as a safe, progressive, clean, comfortable and reliable railway. This philosophy was exemplified by two posters produced in the early 1930s under his direction: *Power* by E.McKnight Kauffer and *Speed* by Alan Rogers. It was his belief that the organisation must be proud of these attributes and should be constantly improving the design and efficiency of its products and services.

Because of this, he started to apply his design management philosophy more broadly to influence major areas such as the design of rolling stock as well as the details of publicity material. He was singularly unimpressed with

Just one year later experimental modifications had already been made to the interior. The close-coupled ceiling mounted lamps had been replaced by light fittings located in the eaves. These illuminated the car interior through glazed panels inserted into an unusual *ladder* frame arrangement. Vertical grabpoles had also made an appearance which stopped clear of the floor surface to aid cleaning – another feature that would appear 70 years later in the refurbished tube stock designs. These ideas were not however implemented for other cars of Cammell Laird stock.

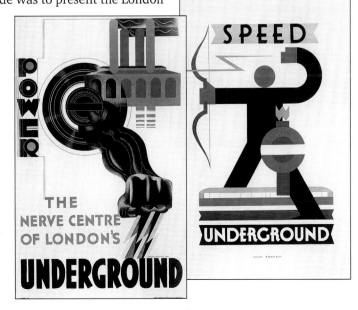

As can be seen in this view of a 1920 Stock trailer car, the door glazing aligned with the car windows with their hinged vent panels, but thicker framing was necessary to accommodate the curvature of the doors. Just visible is the pilot lamp on the centre pillar. Exterior door fault indicator lights were subsequently fitted experimentally to a train of Q Stock and as standard on all R Stock shortly after the end of the Second World War. Door fault indicator lights were fitted to A Stock and all tube cars from 1956 Stock onwards, including 1938 Stock as a modification late in its life. These lights illuminate when any one of the door interlocks is broken on that car so that an unclosed door can be easily located.

the design of these 1920 Stock cars; the upright backs which were applied to the door pocket faces were physically very uncomfortable. They would very soon be upgraded to the new tube stock design standards that were being developed. Thereby one bay of transverse seats was provided in the centre of each half of the car, as well as armrests on the remaining longitudinal seats. These were reupholstered in woollen moquette and the harsh uninviting cement flooring was replaced by wooden slats sometime later.

Pick also started to push through various programmes to ensure that the inherited gate stock vehicles were also improved. The CLR cars were converted to automatic door operation but attempts to similarly convert the LER cars were not satisfactory so there were replaced (see pages 34–35).

This 1936 view of the 1920 Stock on a Bakerloo Line platform at Waterloo shows the bulging sides and thick centre-door pillars. All of these Cammell-Laird built cars were withdrawn in 1939 and stored during the Second World War. Five cars which had been converted to an instruction train in 1948 lasted until 1969, the other 35 having been scrapped between 1946 and 1948.

Above By the mid-1920s, under Pick's direction, the car interiors had been further improved by the incorporation of one bay of transverse seats in the centre of the car and the provision of armrests to the remaining longitudinal seats. These were now trimmed in the Underground Group's standard 'lozenge' moquette material and extra swan-necked lamps were fitted to the top of the window line.

Centre left Detail of part of the revised interior taken in 1925 when new. After this date the Bakerloo Line would inherit the trains from the Piccadilly. The extremely shallow draughtscreen design of these trains obviously gave scant weather protection to knees and thighs during winter months.

Centre right This interior 10 years on in Bakerloo Line service looking rather the worse for wear. The lozenge moquette is still fitted.

Below left Finally, at the very end of its service life in May 1939 just before being withdrawn from service. After only 19 years in service they were clearly well and truly eclipsed by the design standards that were then being set by the 1938 Stock.

STARTING FROM SCRATCH

Right Wooden mock-up being built at the Hampstead line's Golders Green depot and works in 1921. Surprisingly, oval cab windows from the 1920 Stock design continue to be proposed as an alternative solution, despite the problems of poor driver visibility.

Below All six of the prototype cars formed up into two special trains for a press demonstration held in February 1923 on the Piccadilly Line. They were received very favourably. They were variously described as 'tube cars *de luxe*' and 'Underground Pullman specials'. Three of them are to be seen coupled to an ex Great Northern, Piccadilly & Brompton Railway gate stock car and the other three to a car of 1920 Tube Stock. The bogies are fitted with sound deadening shrouds – an initiative of Frank Pick to reduce noise levels. They were not a success and were removed after a short time in service.

Frank Pick foresaw the benefits that a standardised design of tube train would now bring with the large orders that would be required for the replacement of gate stock and enlargement of the system. Extension of the Charing Cross, Euston & Hampstead line from Golders Green to Edgware was planned as was the rebuilding of the City & South London Railway with its ultimate extension through to Morden in Surrey. The two lines were also to be linked via a newly constructed section between Euston and Camden Town and a connection at Kennington.

A wooden mock-up of a control trailer car was built during 1921 by the Underground Group's engineering staff at Golders Green depot. Supported by a considerable number of engineering drawings, this defined the required design approach for a brand new fleet of vehicles. This was a company owned design and performance specification, very similar to today's procedures for the development and procurement of new rolling stock.

Two views of the control trailer vehicle 720 which was built to the Underground Group's own specification by the Gloucester Railway Carriage & Wagon Company. For the first time, two sets of double doors were fitted on all of the trailer cars, but with no passenger doors fitted at the car ends. The struggles of passengers to get out of a packed train via just these double doors was overlooked, and it was not until 1930 that air operated single-leaf doors would be introduced at the ends of trailer cars of what was to become known as the Standard Stock. The oval cab windows had been thankfully abandoned but the untidy arrangement of air hoses, sockets and driving lamps had not as yet progressed from Yerkes vehicles.

The interior of car 720, the colour scheme of which was generally brown and white. Wooden framing was polished mahogany and all of the fittings, including the brackets for the 22 unshaded lamps, were manufactured from bronze with an oxidised copper finish. Seats were covered in moquette with leather armrests and this was the first appearance of the Underground Group's 'lozenge' pattern (see also page 15). This was to become the standard design used throughout the 'twenties and early 'thirties, not only on all of the trains but also the motor buses, trolleybuses and tramcars owned by the Underground Group. A single double sided line diagram was located in the centre of the car. It is strange that this inconvenient location, which had existed on the Edwardian tube vehicles, was still perpetuated since the information was clearly inaccessible to those passengers located at the car ends. It was, however, also offered on all the competing vehicles.

In August 1922 five different manufacturers were invited to produce five trailers and one control trailer, all of an experimental nature, to evaluate a final design for the new rolling stock. The five companies worked to an overall UERL specification but were given a free hand in developing their own solutions in terms of construction and finish apart from respecting some essential basic restraints in the building of tube cars. The control trailer was however designed and built to a detailed specification issued by the UERL's own engineers. All six cars were delivered for evaluation only five months later fully finished and furnished in every respect. This was, by any standards past or present, an astonishing performance.

The production versions of these designs would eventually become known as Standard Tube Stock. They were all operationally compatible from day one – only later, when variations such as electro-pneumatic brakes were added, did compatibility become a problem. Because the manufacturers of the prototype cars all used their own favoured methods of construction, there were predictably (as still would be the case today) many differences of detail between them.

At Pick's insistence, all the prototype cars featured experimental solutions to cut down noise produced from the bogies. Some bizarre materials were used to shroud and clad them such as horse-hide leather, and pulped wood sheeting! These were soon abandoned as they were a fire hazard and the designs a maintenance nightmare.

Trailer car 820 was also built by Gloucester but was substantially different, both externally and internally. Note the differently proportioned windows with their thick mullions.

The interior was particularly elaborate, with 30 lamps fitted, most of which were housed in over-the-top fittings that were pure Victoriana! The handgrips were fashioned from polished mahogany and all of the metal fittings were silver oxidised throughout.

The trailer vehicle 823 built by the Birmingham Railway Carriage & Wagon Company had very elegant proportions, with its frameless spring-balanced windows which were arranged to lower up to 6 inches. Small ventilation scoops fitted snugly under the clerestory eaves, which were designed to force air in rather than extract it. The interior mouldings were of polished mahogany and interior panels were painted French grey. Compared with car 820, the white ceiling had an even stronger Victorian design influence with its moulded details and 30 highly decorated lamp fittings!

Below The exterior of car 824, built by Cammell Laird, showing the leather shrouding over the bogies.

Bottom In contrast to cars 820 and 823, the interior was remarkably forward looking in concept, apart from the odd 'wrought-iron' style of scrollwork detailing that was thought necessary. A blue and gold interior colour scheme was lit by 70 lamps, most of which were housed beneath flush-fitting translucent panels each side of the clerestory.

The exterior and interior of car 821, built by the
Leeds Forge Company. The interior design was
commendably simple with no ornamentation
whatsoever, in order to reduce the cleaning
requirements. Pull down blinds were also fitted and
only 20 light bulbs were used, 18 of these being in
ceiling-mounted glass bowls whilst the other two
were used to illuminate a roof mounted line diagram
in the middle of the car.

Finally, car 822 built by the Metropolitan Carriage, Wagon & Finance Company. The interior had blue upholstered seats and armrests with maple and mahogany panelling. Forty electric lamp fittings were installed, enclosed in spherical domes. Significantly, on this version, the floor was not wood but fire-resisting light coloured fluted rubber, a change in material that would be required after the King's Cross station fire 65 years later.

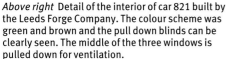

Above right Detail of the interior of car 821 built by the Leeds Forge Company. The colour scheme was green and brown and the pull down blinds can be clearly seen. The middle of the three windows is pulled down for ventilation.

Above End detail emphasising the simple and clean lines of Cammell Laird's design (car 824).

The variety of designs and materials shows the company's commitment to continuing product development rather than just accepting the status quo.

Externally the vehicles were all finished in a handsome livery of vermilion and cream with a black waistband and maroon doors, which was part of the specification. All of the bodies were steel clad except Metro's vehicle which was panelled in aluminium sheet, again anticipating the future by almost 40 years. It also had lightweight rubber strips around the doors providing weather seals and this idea took another 50 years before it really succeeded in service use. There were subtle differences between the cars such as the spacing of saloon windows, the treatment of the one piece cast aluminium doors and the detailing of the ventilation grilles which were either hidden from view by an overhang in the clerestory roof or revealed.

The interior lighting treatment varied enormously for two of them – the offerings from the Gloucester Railway Carriage & Wagon and Birmingham Railway Carriage & Wagon companies featured ornate light fitting clusters which would not have been out of place in later Moscow Metro stations. However in contrast, the Cammell Laird vehicle had fully integrated lighting with individual lamps mounted behind continuous translucent panels; this was a remarkably modern concept and was well ahead of its time. The interior of the car designed and manufactured by the Leeds Forge Company also had a very clean presentation with the lighting realised by ceiling mounted glass bowls and the vehicle from Metropolitan Carriage, Wagon & Finance Company featured spherical bowls partially recessed into the bodywork.

The floor of this particular car was not slatted maple wood but was made from a fire resistant rubberised material, thus anticipating the designs of the refurbishment programme 65 years later! As was to be expected with Pick's influence no doubt being exerted behind the scenes, all of the seats had a high level of comfort and were trimmed in wool moquette. Furthermore the cars from Leeds Forge and Gloucester also had their armrests trimmed in this material – an idea which was to resurface 38 years later on 1960 Stock. All the prototype cars perpetuated transverse line diagrams; a not particularly practical inheritance from the Edwardian Yerkes cars. This would be changed on the first production cars to a longitudinal format above the windows which remains the familiar layout to this day.

These prototype cars were a resounding success and production orders were placed in 1923 with three of the companies (BRCW, CL and MCW) initially for 191 cars which would be used on the Edgware extension of the Hampstead line and for the Morden extension of the reconstructed City & South London Railway.

Such differences that there were centred mainly on slightly different detailing of the draughtscreens (these were either windows with chamfered glass edges which were let into a metal surround, or glazed panels unsupported on one edge as is today's practice) and the manner in which their vertical grabpoles were attached. The painstaking refinement of details such as these developed over time. The production trains also differed from the prototype cars in that the external clerestory section was now broken over the doorways to give extra headroom there.

Two driving motor cars, the upper built by Cammell Laird and the lower by Metropolitan Carriage, Wagon & Finance Company, show the detailed styling differences from the 191 production vehicles that were already delivered by the end of 1923 by these manufacturers and the Birmingham Carriage & Wagon Company. The partially shrouded bogies of 572 show that experiments were still in hand to reduce noises from beneath the car floor. The evolutionary design step has finally been made where the equipment cabinet and passenger compartment share the same body cross section. Note that at this period, car numbers were still in non-Johnston style (although the heavy shading which accompanied the prototype trailer car numbers has been omitted).

Right Marian Stanley, with her father Lord Ashfield, shown alongside a special train of Standard Stock that she had driven from Moorgate to Clapham Common, performing the official opening of the reconstructed City & South London Railway on 1st December 1924.

Above A second batch of stock ordered in 1924 and built by MCW and Birmingham featured these one-piece cast aluminium doors. The ribs and the pronounced housings for the door guide wheels resulted from the production process which required that constant wall thicknesses were retained. All of the driving motor cars built between 1923 and 1928 perpetuated the central door pillar from the 1920 Stock which always was a hindrance when entering and leaving, particularly in rush hour conditions at stations where traffic on and off was equally heavy. The pillars were considered necessary to preserve the torsional rigidity of the driving motor cars to compensate for the massive weight of the equipment chamber.

Right Front end view of a 1923 motor car as originally built by MCW. The train set numbers, destination blind position, headlights, air pipe and electrical connections would all be subsequently repositioned.

A typical interior from the 1923 build, this one manufactured by MCW. Until 1933 and London Transport days, the seating moquette was the Underground Group's standard 'lozenge' pattern which was also used in the motor buses, trolleybuses and tramcars owned by the Group.

The major external styling advance that these trains possessed when compared with every previous tube stock type was, that for the first time ever, the cross section of the cab and the louvred equipment cabinet behind the driver was now the same as the cross sectional profile of the passenger carrying part of the car. It seems obvious that this should be the case but all their predecessors show an awkward visual discontinuity between these two functional elements. The reason for this was most probably due to the fact that on the CLR motor cars as originally built, the wooden saloon was conceived like a body sitting on a chassis, but the equipment area and cab were effectively like the engine and driver's position on a bus and thus naturally part of this chassis. Although saloon bodies were constructed in steel on the cars for the Yerkes lines from 1906 onwards, it still took a full twenty years to alter this stagnant design mindset.

The cab design of the earliest build of 1923 looked scarcely different from the Edwardian Yerkes gate stock cars with its clerestory roof section projecting through to the front, the marker lights spread across the cab face and the same shape of the cab windows. It would appear that the destination blind displays were not a success at the time so there was a return to destination plates. Since these were very heavy a more convenient location was used under the offside window (next to the majority of station platforms). Thus a successful cleaning up of the appearance resulted from this re-appraisal of the frontal layout whereby a marker light display was now neatly incorporated with the destination plates set above inside a window. The treatment of these functions not only set the pattern for all of the subsequent build, but also would be used on the next generation of tube stock as well. The earliest cars of standard stock used the ornate 3-dimensional car numbers which were a carry-over from Victorian and Edwardian graphic styles used by the railways generally in Britain.

The exterior and interior of cars from the 1926 build produced by Metropolitan which were to set the definitive style of these trains right up to the last orders of 1934. The cleaned-up cab front was a substantial improvement visually, with the simple marker light cabinet integrated with the destination box. Cars from the earlier 1923 and 1925 builds would also be eventually updated to this same design. The interior view shows the draughtscreens with glazed panels unsupported on the outside edge, fully upholstered leather armrests and lozenge seating moquette. This was now to be the definitive interior design for all of the Underground Group's vehicles.

Until the mid-1920s it was, as we have seen, the Underground Group's usual practice to issue a general specification (now called a performance specification) for its rolling stock requirements and leave the design details to the manufacturers. However, when the Group developed its own experimental and research facilities at Acton Works, it was able to monitor and control more carefully the standards of their output. They even began manufacturing new trains themselves in 1928 through a subsidiary company, the Union Construction & Finance Company based at Feltham in Middlesex where London United Tramways Feltham tramcars and the bodies for the first London trolleybuses were also built. The versions of Standard Stock built by this concern were identifiable by having a slight curvature to the lower bodyside.

Other train builders naturally shouted 'foul' at this move towards a monopoly supply arrangement by the Group and the UCC was wound up only five years later, following the formation of London Transport. The terms of LT's constitution prohibited the manufacture of any future rolling stock for its own use other than prototypes.

Over the years, there were further minor amendments to the livery that reflected the prevailing attitudes of the time. One example was the application of the Line name as dedicated graphics on the sides of vehicles delivered in the mid-thirties. Although some cars stayed on the same lines right up to 1966, others transferred onto other lines and so this experiment proved to be short lived. The concept was brought back again 60 years later in the mid 1990s on trains as part of the corporate external livery programme. However, this time it was to be a more manageable and flexible solution with line identity labels placed in the lower half of some windows.

Air operated single leaf doors at each end were finally provided in 1930 on these experimental trailer cars by the UCC. Although eight seats were lost in the process, the added safety and convenience for passengers who were now able to enter and leave a crowded train far more easily was incalculable. All builds from 1931 onwards would have this feature. The one-piece cast aluminium doors were also now changed to a construction method that is still familiar today, being skinned with sheet metal (steel) panelling. On production cars the two wide windows of the end bays would be re-arranged to three, with similar proportions to those of the centre bay.

Bottom Interior view of one of the these prototype cars showing that the car end transverse seats had now disappeared. Another important development that greatly improved operational safety and convenience of use was the fact that the guard's control panels on the 1931/1934 driving motors would be now attached to the end wall for the first time, thus enabling the guard to operate the buttons whilst facing them and looking towards the train. (Previously the guard had to operate a panel behind him if looking towards the front.) This also provided a guard's gangway which was fully and safely usable by passengers. The interior shows an early departure in seat covering from the standard lozenge pattern; somebody obviously thought it a good idea to use a floral pattern, inspired by contemporary furniture fabrics. Frank Pick presumably supported the change because there would be many more similar types of seat patterns in use up to 1936, but in the same year he was to spearhead a more rational and pragmatic approach to the design of seat patterns for rolling stock.

In 1930 a batch of cars was built to replace the ex LER-LNWR Watford Joint Stock cars (see introduction), most of which were just over ten years old but were noticeably slower than the standard stock trains which had been operating the local service between Queens Park and Elephant & Castle. In order to distinguish this new batch from the locals, a blue stripe was added to the sides of the Watford bound trains through the window line. In 1934, the Bakerloo Line name was added to the body below the waist line in a similar style to 'London Transport' which was moved from the centre of the body to the left hand end, to balance the additional line name.

Bottom Just before Coronation Day on 12th May 1937, trains of various vintages of Standard Stock are lined up abreast at Golders Green depot. They are being prepared to help carry the extra thousands who came to London to see that great event.

Below One of the 1906 French built gate stock cars converted in 1921 to run with the Cammell Laird trailers. This involved enclosing the open platform and providing centrally located air operated doors.

Centre and bottom One of the original American Car & Foundry Company gate stock trailer cars, which was converted about 1925 to air door operation. The door at the left end of the car was a revolving one and was operated by an air engine under the floor.

The Standard Stock, with its modern lines and air-operated sliding doors for passengers, was ideally suited to the developing Underground of the 1920s. There were a number of different designs still dating from the days of separate railway companies, which were not old enough to send to the scrapyard; many of these still with gated ends. We have seen how conversion to air doors not only reduced the number of staff needed on each train but also meant that less time was needed at each station for passengers to board and alight. On the trailers that were converted to run with 1920 Stock, the doors were edged with a soft canvas material; this was later changed to rubber, which is still in use today.

In 1926, conversion of the existing rolling stock on the Central London Railway

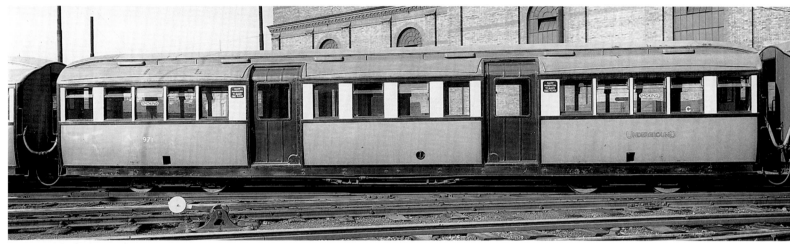

Top A rebuilt Central London Railway train alongside a brand new train of Standard Stock destined for the Morden – Edgware Line. While the Central London cab front gives away the train's age, not much more surgery would have been required to radius the cab window tops and install a one piece communicating door.

Above Photograph taken in 1926 to show the reconstruction of the original Central London Railway gate-stock cars to meet the new standards which had been developed. Note the complete new car ends, new door openings, renewed framing and panels obscuring the old bodysides. Although successful, the work proved very costly. The 24 motor cars built by Brush in 1915 for the CLR (see Chapter One) were similarly converted so that their appearance and interior features were consistent with these trailer cars.

The interiors of these rebuilt cars were made to closely resemble the contemporary Standard Stock interior design to a remarkable degree of detail. It demonstrates Pick's drive to realise a standardised marketing approach for the company's products and services.

had to be carried out because its smaller tunnel dimensions and its different current collection system did not permit the introduction of these new standardised trains. Pick insisted, however, that this conversion work should also include a comprehensive remodelling of the original inherited interiors of these trains in order to be fully complementary with the finally resolved designs. The accompanying photographs show how successfully this work was carried out. The required finance to remodel and enlarge these tunnels and also to convert the line to the standard LT fourth rail system was finally made available as part of the 1935-40 New Works Programme, and these Edwardian tube trains, albeit substantially altered, still remained in service on the Central Line until June 1939.

STANDARD STOCK
IN LATER LIFE

Right Evocative photograph taken in early 1951 of a passenger seated in a corner of a Standard Stock car. This was part of a series commissioned by *Picture Post* magazine to illustrate an article describing a typical 24 hours on the Underground system. The seat moquette pattern was designed in 1945 by Enid Marx, who named it *Shield*.

One of the 340 cars of Standard Stock extensively refurbished in 1947 for use on the Central Line, having been stored in the open for the duration of the Second World War.

Standard Stock became the largest group of any particular design of stock to operate on the Underground system, for 1,466 cars would be built over a 12 year period between 1922 and 1934. During their lives they were used on every London Underground line of their time, including the western branches of the surface District and the Stanmore branch of the Metropolitan. The essential and familiar characteristics that we recognise in the tube trains of today such as the arrangement of their air operated sliding doors and their comfortable, moquette covered seating made their first appearance in these vehicles. Furthermore, since the last complete trains of the stock remained in service on the Northern City line until 1966, they played an intrinsic role in the evolving social history of London over four tumultuous decades. For instance, in the realm of women's fashions, the same vehicles would have carried cloche hatted flappers in the 1920s, WAAFs, WRNSs and ATS girls during the Second World War, girls clad in 1940s utility clothing and the new look styles culminating with the Mary Quant Swinging London fashions of 1964!

As a testimony to their excellent build quality, 43 cars were sold on to the then Southern Region of British Railways in 1966 to run on newly electrified lines on the Isle of Wight where they were operated for a further twenty three years, being finally displaced by refurbished 1938 Tube Stock in 1989. The oldest of them was by then over 65 years old! A handful of these were then repatriated back to the mainland where one of them was repainted into the original livery of those first prototype cars for a Morden Depot open day in 1990, to celebrate the centenary of the C&SLR. It is hoped that one day the best of these ex-island cars, together with some ex works personnel carriers may be restored to represent once again a working 7-car set.

Two cars of F Stock when new, forming a train with some ancient looking District Railway B Stock cars dating from the beginning of the 20th Century. Note the chains between vehicles (an idea inherited from the New York Metro system) to prevent passengers falling between them, a concept – albeit using different materials – that was reintroduced on the Underground fleet in the late 1990s. The indicators by the centre doors were to show those stations at which the train was not stopping – they were all displayed in this posed view. Similar display boards would be fitted to surface stock trains up to the beginning of the Second World War. The overall styling of these trailer cars is very similar to today's trains on Metropolitan Line services, built 40 years later.

Below left The somewhat forbidding appearance of the front of an F Stock train with its distinctive oval cab windows.

Below right A train operator's nightmare – a claustrophobic so-called functional cab interior with appalling outward vision. Hapless drivers would have to tolerate this ergonomic disaster for some 44 years before the last cars were finally scrapped.

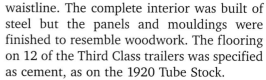

SURFACE STOCK TRAINS

The year 1920 signalled the beginning of the end of the District Line's American inspired surface stock designs that had been inherited from the Yerkes era, which, it is said, had been closely modelled on the trains of the Brooklyn Elevated Line.

100 cars of the heavy, all steel bodied F Class, built by the Metropolitan Carriage, Wagon & Finance Company in Birmingham, started to enter service in December of that year. Externally they were characterised by the same oval cab windows as the contemporary Cammell-Laird tube control trailers, an odd choice because this was a modish design solution, certainly not fit for purpose because they restricted considerably the driver's outside view. The Berlin Underground also had vehicles with this feature that were built in the mid 1920s and one of these trains survives today, forming part of their own historical collection. All of the London Underground's vehicles were, however, scrapped after spring 1963 when the last train of the type ran in service on the Uxbridge branch of the Metropolitan Line.

Three pairs of hand worked double doors, narrower than those used today, were provided on each bodyside, subsequently being converted to air operation in 1938-40. The body width at 9ft 7in was eleven inches greater than the previous wooden bodied vehicles, and was only one inch narrower than today's A Stock vehicles, built 40 years later.

The side elevation was also very similar to A Stock with a similar crease at the waistline. The complete interior was built of steel but the panels and mouldings were finished to resemble woodwork. The flooring on 12 of the Third Class trailers was specified as cement, as on the 1920 Tube Stock.

Frank Pick was not happy with the original interior design of these cars because he recognised that the all-steel interior produced a cold, unwelcoming appearance, partly due to the fact that the seats were originally covered in rexine material. To brighten up the cars, he procured the services of a well-known artist to plan new interior colour schemes and get more life into the upholstery pattern in order to give them a warmer appearance. He also instigated experiments to try to reduce the noise level from the powerful motors. The picture opposite and that on the following page show how these interiors were later transformed as a result of his direct influence.

Left The interior as built. An ugly and unwelcoming environment with its forest of poles, rexine covered seats with no armrests, and linoleum covered concrete floor – and this is in the First Class section!

Below Again First Class, but certainly much better! The revised interior developed as a result of Frank Pick commissioning a prominent artist who introduced a warmer colour scheme and friendlier seat pattern. Armrests were also added.

Interior of Third Class section of revised
1920 Stock. Plush inviting moquette-covered
upholstery using the Underground Group's *lozenge*
pattern with armrests was fitted and the interior
simplified and *opened out* by removing all of the full
depth grabpoles.

The Underground Group also ordered several batches of cars of different designs from 1923 through to 1935 for use on the District Line. These were the G Class (1923), K (1927), L (1931), M and N (1935). Eventually they were converted to run with Q Stock (1938) and all then became generically known as 'Q' Stock. They followed the Underground tradition of being remarkably long lived, some of the oldest of them remained in service until 1971; almost 50 years of continuous service to Londoners! One of the original 1923 motor cars is preserved today in London's Transport Museum.

Not unexpectedly, the first series of 50, built in 1923 by the Gloucester Railway Carriage & Wagon Company, had many of the design features of the contemporary

Above One of the 1923 G Class motor cars in its Underground Group livery. The maroon paintwork of the hand operated passenger doors was repeated on the driver's centre door. The manner in which the clerestory roof ran through to the front, and the arched cab windows, closely follow the style that had now been established for tube stock.

Below The interior of one of these cars. In every respect it was a *big brother* to the equivalent standard tube stock design of 1923, with identical treatments of grabpoles, draughtscreens, lamps and, of course, the same seat moquette pattern.

One of the 101 Birmingham built K Class motor cars when new in 1929. The smoother profiling of the cab front is readily apparent and the downward curving of the clerestory roof to meet the cab top is an obvious visual improvement. There is now a close affinity with the 1927 tube stock as a result of the similar marker light box and integrated glazed destination display. Unlike contemporary tube trains, doors were still painted in contrasting maroon on the first deliveries, though this changed to matching red during delivery as shown in the two K class cars in this formation.

tube stock with arched tops to the cab windows and the clerestory roof section running out to the cab front. They were boxy in the extreme, with vertical sides and an almost completely flat front and were fitted with hand operated doors. Standardisation of design was also being forced through by Pick on these surface stock cars because the interior closely resembled the tube stock of the same year with the identical design of draughtscreen, light fittings and moquette pattern being used.

In 1927 he was able to influence more effectively the appearance of the next order of 101 K Class cars, built by the Birmingham Railway Carriage & Wagon Company and delivered between 1928 and 1930. These were considerably better looking since they had a less box-like appearance due to much smoothing of the contours and curving the end of the clerestory roof down to meet the top of the cab. The cleaning up of the front end of standard tube stock that has already been mentioned was also followed through with a similar grouping of the five marker lights contained in a single panel below an integrated glazed destination display box. (Previously destination plates had been inserted into brackets on the front of the car.)

Interior of a K Class vehicle. Again, the detailing now corresponds in all respects with the equivalent tube stock car. The standardised Underground Group look has, by now, been fully established across all rail vehicles in its ownership.

Opposite page Detail of the first seat bay showing the simply resolved design of the passenger alarm handle mounted on top of the grabpole.

An L Class motor car built in 1931 by the Underground Group's own Union Construction Company.

The interior design was updated in parallel with the developments being achieved in the equivalent tube stock which now featured the more open fully glazed draughtscreens. We can see how the Underground Group through Frank Pick (who became Managing Director in 1928) was now, in today's parlance, insisting on and achieving a policy of continuing product development and improvement.

These were to be followed in 1931 by the L Class (built by UCC, the Group's own manufacturing subsidiary) and in 1935 by the M and N classes, which were more luxurious in character. First Class compartments were re-introduced and the cars also featured plusher seating throughout as well as inlaid ebonised wooden trim panels let into the draughtscreens. By 1931, the Underground Group's standard lozenge moquette seat pattern was being replaced by a variety of home furnishing textile

An L Class trailer car interior, looking through the fully open partition door to the First Class coupé. The inlaid ebonised wood treatment on the inside faces of the draughtscreens was to remain a feature on subsequent types of surface stock cars built for the District Line over the next 28 years.

Facing page The harlequin seat pattern is another early departure from the standardised lozenge design; a development which is apparent across tube and surface stock cars from 1931 onwards.

A 6-car train of the 1935 built M Stock, the first surface stock design to include trains fitted with air operated passenger doors from new, operating on the Hammersmith & City Line.

designs and these were now making an appearance on both the surface and tube stock cars. Surprisingly only two trains of the M stock (built by Metro-Cammell, as MCW were now called), had air operated doors fitted by the manufacturer and these were complemented by passenger operated selective door open buttons. This was the first time that these had ever been fitted on any Underground train although they were subsequently taken out of use. This feature would eventually reappear on District Line trains 43 years later.

These particular trains were the last clerestory roofed vehicles to be built in the UK, the last of a line that went back to the earliest days of this century with their American design influence. The vehicles that were to follow them, which are described in the next chapter, were to arguably become the most stylish and distinctive fleet of surface stock trains ever built for the Underground.

Close up view showing the door control buttons and the short lived *Metropolitan Line* branding of the trains, of which the Hammersmith & City formed part until given its own identity (and colour) in 1990.

METROPOLITAN LINE

Have you seen the
NEW TRAIN
now running on the Hammersmith and City Line?

Different Windows
Different Ventilators
Different Seats
Different Doors
Different Brakes

and the new **PUSH TO OPEN**

Automatic Door Release

4403

Left The flush fitting windows were a pleasing design feature of these trains.

Below Interior of M Stock trailer car. The externally hung destination panels were housed in compartments fitted onto the draughtscreens. Unlike today, the railway passengers of the time could be trusted to leave them well alone (with the additional fear, as laid down in the bye-laws, of a hefty penalty if tampered with)!

CHAPTER THREE

The years 1933 to 1939

Herbert Morrison, photographed in 1929 when he became Labour's Minister of Transport.

In 1929, Herbert Morrison, the Minister of Transport in the then newly elected Labour Government, recommended the creation of a Transport Board for London to be run on similar lines to the recently established BBC and Central Electricity Generating Board. Consolidation and co-ordination were the key words used in reports of that Government's plan to unify the capital's tramway, underground and omnibus services because "no lasting solution of the dual problem of the congestion of the streets and the provision of proper facilities for travelling could be found unless further steps are taken to eliminate uneconomic and unnecessary competition."

A further change to a National Government in 1931 removed Morrison from office, but the London Passenger Transport Bill was eventually passed and the new authority came into being on 1st July 1933. The full support of Lord Ashfield, Chairman of the Underground Group of Companies, which owned two thirds of the operations that were taken over by the LPTB, had been essential in driving the bill through. He and his deputy, Frank Pick would continue to dominate London Transport during the thirties. Between them, they possessed more than half a century's experience with the Underground group, together they made 'a formidable pair' to quote Herbert Morrison. Their combined administrative abilities, and Pick's special concern for the highest standards of design in every aspect of the Board's operations from stations and vehicles down to ticket machines and litter bins, helped to shape a transport system that was to become the envy of the world.

It was a period in which Frank Pick was able to influence and control fully every aspect of how London Transport presented itself to its passengers and staff. Nothing would go forward for further development without his personal approving signature on a drawing or document and two secretaries were kept busy ceaselessly typing out his memoranda to every branch of the organisation, to ensure that he got what he wanted. And so it was that these few years saw the development of train types that would be the envy of the world in terms of their design and comfort. The last few trains of what were to become the classic 1938 stock were to see a life of 50 years in the service of Londoners, for in order to cope with a continuing increase in traffic from the mid to late 1980s, five complete trains were immaculately restored back to their original appearance, both inside and out. They had become the bench mark of what a London tube train is and should look like; their design influence continuing through to 1983. However, during these 45 years, ensuing train designs became increasingly devoid of the uniquely felicitous touches that made the 1938 trains so special and which endeared them to the travelling public.

On and from July 1st the following undertakings are transferred to the London Passenger Transport Board:

RAILWAYS
Metropolitan District Railway
London Electric Railway
City and South London Railway
Central London Railway
Metropolitan Railway

TRAMWAYS
London County Council, Barking, Bexley, Croydon, Dartford, East Ham, Erith, Ilford, Leyton, Walthamstow, West Ham, London United, Metropolitan Electric, South Metropolitan Electric

OMNIBUSES AND COACHES
London General, London General Country Services, Overground, Tilling & British Automobile Traction, Green Line Coaches

Notice will be given as certain other undertakings are absorbed

All inquiries should be addressed to

LONDON PASSENGER TRANSPORT BOARD
55, Broadway, Westminster, S.W.1

Telephone: VICtoria 6800
Telegrams: Passengers Sowest London

The experimental streamlined cab that had been grafted onto the front of a Standard Stock control trailer car in January 1933, photographed five months later.

TUBE STOCK TRAINS

As we have already seen, the external appearance of the Standard Stock cars, produced between 1923 and 1934, was largely a development of that of the Hungarian and French vehicles built in the Edwardian era. Similar features were the manner in which the connecting pipe work was slung in an expedient fashion onto the front of the cab, and the method in which the clerestory roof section was also run out to the front. The car's electrical equipment still took up one quarter of the space of the motor car. It is true to say that their overall appearance was similar to other contemporary electric metro trains in Europe and America and certainly did not possess a really unique style. This was all changed on the 1938 Stock trains when a painstaking cleaning up of the appearance took place; function drove these changes but they were skilfully married to a fresh, clean-lined approach to the train's styling. The cab front was smoothed and simplified with the various hoses and conduits of previous types no longer hung on as appendages to the cab front. For the first time, a major technical leap forward in equipment design had enabled the electrical traction equipment to be completely housed below the floor of a driving motor car. This was made possible by the development of a new small format traction motor which could be installed in each bogie. But dramatic as this engineering and design breakthrough was, it was born out of an even more adventurous development; that of the 1935 streamlined trains.

In 1934, William S. Graff-Baker, as deputy to W. A. Agnew, Chief Mechanical Engineer (Railways), was in charge of new car design and so the development of all rail vehicles during this period, both tube and surface stock, was his responsibility. He had a vision of a high speed tube train (with all cars fitted with motors) which would be fitted out with luxurious Green Line coach type seating, and he wanted its external appearance to reflect this high speed aspiration. The then newly formed LPTB wanted new, universal tube and surface stock trains to replace remaining old ones (especially on the Metropolitan and Central Lines) and for the planned line extensions.

W. S. Graff-Baker

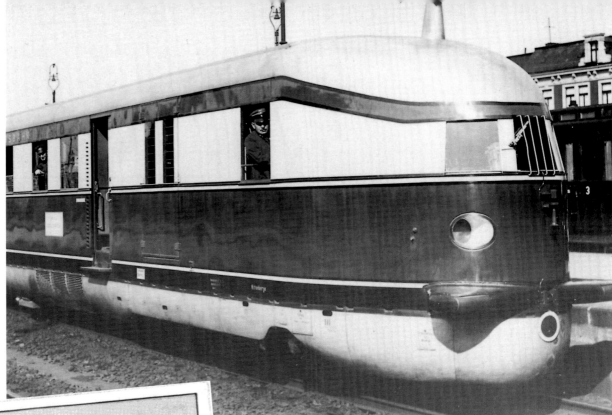

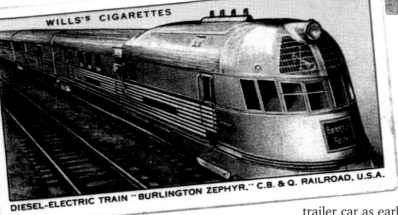

Streamlining was very much the spirit of the time in both Europe and America. The high speed diesel electric railcar The Flying Hamburger had first entered service on the Berlin to Hamburg route in 1933 and the all-stainless-steel Burlington Zephyr was a notable exhibit at the 1934 Century of Progress exposition in Chicago. Not only were these trains fully described in the technical magazines of the day but their exciting visual images were also in common currency since they both featured in a popular set of cigarette cards!

It is therefore not surprising that a streamlined cab had already been grafted onto the front of a standard stock control trailer car as early as January 1933. This was then the subject of test running for six months at night on the Piccadilly Line before being converted back to the normal design. The experiment, with a strangely bulbous, insect-like cab front visually at such odds with the rest of the car, became the inspiration for something rather more exciting and adventurous. These were the eighteen cars ordered in 1935 and delivered through to the end of 1937, now known as the 1935 Tube Stock but then referred to as 'High speed trains'.

Top The high speed diesel-electric railcar set that commenced scheduled services between Hamburg and Berlin in May 1933.

Above The Chicago, Burlington & Quincy Railroad's all-stainless-steel *Burlington Zephyr* of 1934 which featured in a popular cigarette card series.

Below left New York, New Haven & Hartford Railroad's *Comet* ran the 43 miles between Boston and Providence in the same number of minutes.

Below right Gulf, Mobile & Northern Railroad's diesel electric *Rebel* travelled 751 miles (1,209 km) between St Louis and New Orleans in 22 hours.

The painting opposite is of a model presented to Underground managers in January 1935 to illustrate what they would be getting; this showed two single leaf doors per side and a strongly art deco inspired cream flash running down to the front of a streamlined cab. However, what was significant was the fact that this showed passenger seating right up to the wall of the driver's cab, which would be effected by all of the control gear and motors being placed below the floor. There is no record to indicate that there was great enthusiasm concerning the extra number of passengers

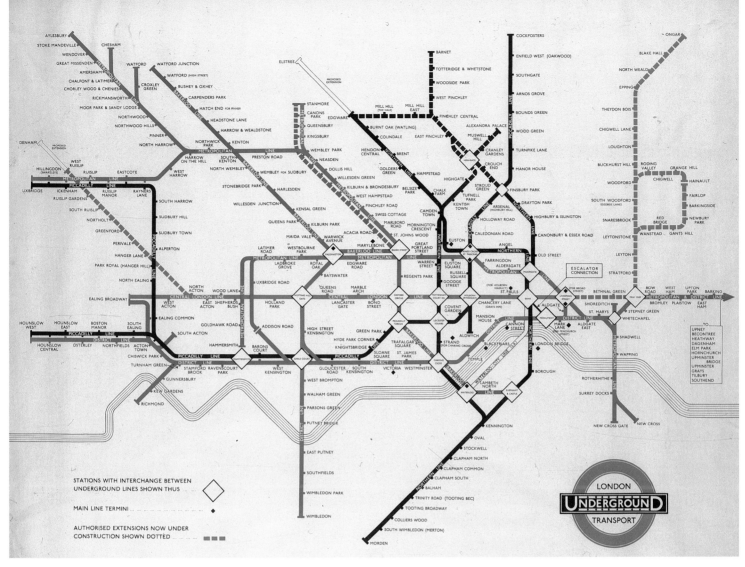

that a driving motor car could now carry as a result of this major technical breakthrough. All we know is that Frank Pick himself disliked the livery as well as the appearance of the rounded ends because of the large gap that would be formed when these were brought together in a train formation. The then Engineering Committee, headed by Mr Agnew, also disliked the gap and the sum of £25,496 for the completion of a 2-car prototype train was withheld; the excuse being given that they first wanted to see for themselves the effect of the obligatory raised floor which numerous motored bogies would require before proceeding any further. A further submission by Graff-Baker, now CME (Railways) four months later – W. A. Agnew having in the meantime retired – was successful. It was based on improved operating costs and passenger

Top Underground map of 1937 showing planned extensions to the Northern and Central Lines for which new trains were needed.

Above Painting of the model that was shown to Underground managers in January 1935 showing the two single-leaf doors per side and the *deco* inspired angled cream flash.

One of the experimental streamlined cars being built at the works of Metro-Cammell in Birmingham.

amenities which these trains would deliver over existing trains in service on the Hampstead Line, now part of the Northern Line. The completely inadequate single doors, two per bodyside, were replaced by conventional double and single passenger doors. These were now more smoothly integrated into the bodysides than had been achieved on the Standard Stock cars by the use of a sleeker radiused cross section which delineated the door apertures and neatly related the doors to the bodysides and roof. This distinctive contouring not only enabled improved cleaning performance to be achieved by mechanical washers but it also was to become a hallmark of the unique style of London's tube trains and was continued on all of the cars built up to 1983. The cream flash had also now disappeared but the streamlined front was retained on all but one train and, about this, more later.

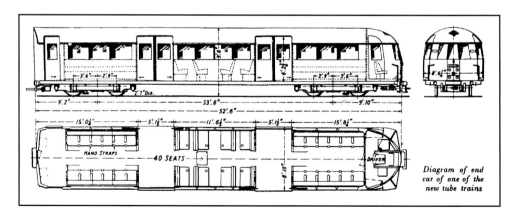

Diagram of end car of one of the new tube trains showing the driver's seating position.

Diagram of end car of one of the new tube trains

Correspondence between the LPTB and the Railway Inspectorate indicates that there were serious doubts about the desirability of the streamlined ends. A model of the streamlined driver's cab was the subject of a meeting on 6th February 1936 at which Colonel Mount of the Railway Inspectorate expressed concern about the poorer facilities for detrainment of passengers through the front cab in an emergency and the potential for people to fall into the large space between coupled streamlined units. Large guard rails were added to the design following this meeting. To improve ease of

exit through the front, the original cab door design, which slid back into the driving cab, was replaced by a hinged door with some increase in the dimensions of the opening.

A further inspection was made on 13th February, in the company of Mr J. P. Thomas, operating manager, and Graff-Baker. The emergency exit arrangements were now satisfactory and further consideration was given to the gap between units.

The report on this meeting also indicates that the first of the proposed streamline stock had originally been intended for the Central London Line, whose positive rail was close to the platform and another potential hazard for anyone falling while attempting to board the train. The Railway Inspectorate was subsequently informed that transfer of Standard Stock from the Morden–Edgware Line to the Central and use of the new stock on the Morden–Edgware was being considered.

The Ministry of Transport remained unhappy, however. In a letter to J. P. Thomas dated 17th February they said: 'We are not convinced of the necessity for streamlining tube stock; we think the construction will cost more, it will not have the slightest traffic earning value, and the public would certainly prefer 16 additional seats in a crowded 8-coach train'. As already mentioned, Frank Pick disliked the streamlined front end also. J. P. Thomas expressed the view that streamlining was a 'passing phase'. There seemed little or no enthusiasm for it other than from Graff-Baker.

In the same 17th February letter from the Ministry, Colonel Mount suggested that 'one or two of the three new trains be constructed with a "normal" end, instead of having a streamlined one, to each coach'. On 11th March, J. P. Thomas replied that following this suggestion, the Board had agreed that 'one of the four new trains shall, by way of comparison, have the same type of blunt ends as the Standard tube stock'.

The first 2-car unit, as part of the first 6-car train, delivered at the end of 1936 with the significant numbers 10000 and 11000, even possessed a feature that would be highly desirable on Underground trains a full 60 years later and which has only recently been introduced in the cabs of refurbished 1973 Stock, namely a form of air-conditioning.

Above Interior of one of the cabs. Only 12 years separate this prototype streamlined 2-car set from the first public appearance of the Standard Stock; an amazing development mirrored only by the equally dramatic design development of airliners in the United States over the same period. The top photograph shows how smoothly the doors were integrated into the bodysides. This treatment was to become a unique stylistic feature of London's tube trains for almost another 40 years. Air conditioning was fitted to this unit, hence the absence of opening windows. A trial of air conditioning had been first carried out in a Standard Stock car in December 1934.

The dramatic front end of the streamliners, with three windscreen wipers, completely flush front and side cab access doors and the first appearance of the 'feather' air intake grille. The introduction of auto-couplers was a major influence in enabling the front to be cleaned up in the manner shown. Note that destination blinds have been re-introduced and that the polished lamp bracket doubles as a door handle (this idea did not work in practice and it had to be changed).

A view of the GEC equipped streamlined 2-car unit 10006/11006. This has conventional opening windows instead of air-conditioning. Note that on some streamlined units including this one the front cab door was cut into the roof profile.

Another notable aspect was a central driving position on a padded, reversible armchair type seat which once again, 60 years on, was specified on new trains for London such as Heathrow Express.

The appearance of these trains with their boldly sculptured prows and raked back cab windows has compelling style and panache even to this day and their image was more befitting a high speed inter-urban rail car than a metro car serving the centre of London and its outer suburbs. A particularly stylish touch was the ventilation grille at the front of the domed roof in the form of a feather, a true art-deco detail. The press, both local and national, loved these new trains, calling them 'streamlined wonders' and eulogising about the three main features – air conditioning, quieter and smoother

The GEC equipped unit 10006/11006 featured a simplified screen design with the glass edge exposed, but with a rather crude mounting bracket for fixing the grabpole to the draughtscreen panel. The windows have reverted to the more familiar hinged ventilator panel. Moquette design on the seats is the first example of fabric that was commissioned by Christian Barman, then Publicity Officer under Frank Pick, which did not owe its origins to printed fabric designs. This was *Belsize*, designed by Enid Marx in 1936.

ride and rapid acceleration (2mph per second). The interiors featured the first application of the sprung ball-ended strap hangers which would become a standardised solution for the next 50 years, as opposed to the those of the closed-loop stirrup variety as previously used on the Standard Stock. Very convenient for passengers were the 'handed' line diagrams over the longitudinal seating so that the information related to the direction of travel (a feature which is often still requested by passengers, but is not possible in trains that are reversible, such as on the Central, Circle and Piccadilly lines). The ceilings featured a highly reflective surface of parabolic section with individual cast glass luminaires shaped and positioned to maximise the light spread onto them. The moquette design in the first unit was a bold art-deco pattern, totally redolent of that exotic style. The design of armrests was however a carry-over from the previous generations of Standard Stock. Two other moquette patterns were also used on subsequent vehicles built under this particular contract, and the interior view of the GEC equipped unit shows another, more prosaic pattern which was also used.

The draughtscreens were different on the first unit because of the forced ventilation equipment that was fitted. There were two sheets of glass separated by a gap, with air being drawn in from the top. This resulted in the uncomfortable detailing (both visually and ergonomically) of the framed edge of the glass and the proximity of the handrail. Since the subsequent vehicles were fitted with hinged ventilator panels, the draughtscreens on these cars reverted to a more simple solution. In truth the sculptured front ends had no relevance to performance. It was always acknowledged that there would be no wind-cheating characteristics below 45mph. The style was chosen because Graff-Baker thought that it was appropriate and was in harmony with the general expectation of what a brand new generation of tube trains should look like. The central driving configuration was also never liked by the train drivers. Effective sealing of the hinged door of the cab was particularly difficult and drivers must have found the resulting draughts a constant annoyance. Indeed this remains a technical problem that is very difficult to resolve satisfactorily even with today's technology and materials.

Facing page Interior of the first streamlined experimental unit of 1935 Stock. Since this featured an early form of air-conditioning with the equipment supplied by Frigidaire Limited mounted underneath the car, none of the windows have opening sections. Window frames are chromium plated and sprung ball ended strap hangers made their début on these trains. The sharp corners of the draughtscreens and the over-elaborate double vertical poles created by the draughtscreen framing in close proximity to the grabpoles are uncomfortable visual details, in contrast to the smooth transition of the seat riser panel to accommodate extra operating equipment at the point nearest the doors. Note the distinctive *deco* upholstery pattern, coloured in pink, charcoal grey and cream, and the handed line diagrams.

Below Side elevation of the first 2-car set, numbers 10000 and 11000.

THE MIDDLESEX COUNTY TIMES,
SATURDAY, NOVEMBER 21, 1936

NEW STREAMLINED TUBE TRAIN

Additional Comfort for Passengers

EVEN FOR STRAP-HANGERS

I rocketed through Ealing and Acton on Tuesday afternoon in the very latest thing in Tube trains (writes a "Middlesex County Times" reporter). Picking up from an acceleration of two miles per hour per second, she slid noiselessly out of North-fields depot and ran smoothly at an even 45 miles an hour as far as Acton Town.

This new train, one of four which will shortly be put into service by London Transport, is the very last word in streamlining. Its graceful lines, sweeping in a compact curve from end to end, have been specially designed to reduce wind-resistance when running at high speed on open sections of line.

Increased acceleration and retardation will mean that the train will reach faster maximum speeds between stations situated some distance apart.

In every way the comfort of the passenger has been studied in this new design. Formerly, special compartments had to be provided on the trains to accommodate electrical equipment. By placing the equipment beneath the floor of the first coach all the space within the train—with the exception of the driver's tiny cab—can now be used for seating passengers.

QUIETER TRAVELLING.

At long last it is going to be possible to carry on a connected conversation. Special gears and wheels with new silencing devices have been employed. Added to that the interior of the car sheeting has been sprayed with a noise-deadening composition.

Windows are flush with the outside panels of the car. Pillars between the windows are smaller than usual, and are triangular in section, thus enlarging the passenger's outlook and, when seen from the outside, the train appears to have one window extending through its length.

A continuous supply of fresh air will be filtered into each car. This supply is controlled thermostatically and during runs on open stretches will be heated to an even temperature.

There is more comfort, too, for the driver. He will sit in the middle of a semi-circular cab, with a clear view ahead, maintained in wet weather by three automatic windscreen wipers, which will sweep clear the whole of the glass.

There is one other novel feature which deserves mention—the new adjustable hand-grip. The diminutive strap-hanger, who has had in the past to travel to town standing on his toes, will now be able to read his newspaper in comfort.

Above The unit on a test track between South Ealing and Acton Town in November 1936.

Above inset Giving answers to every schoolboy's inquisitive mind, this issue of *Modern Wonder* magazine was published on 20th August 1938. The cover was devoted to the workings of the streamlined tube trains and the artist, L. Ashwell Wood, will be no stranger to readers of the *Eagle* published 12 years later, for he continued to practise his skills with cut-out mechanical illustrations, including one of the successor 1938 Stock.

Streamlined stock on its first service journey on the Piccadilly Line, 8th April 1937. All the trains of 1935 Stock worked on this line until 1940, albeit somewhat erratically.

All of the 1935 trains were put in storage at Cockfosters depot during the Second World War but strangely, during the height of wartime activity, two streamlined cabs were redesigned to both place the driver on the conventional left hand side and also to allow the train to be driven standing up, not possible with the original design of cab. The only external difference was that the cab windows extended into the roof dome but the appearance was certainly compromised. The drivers were still not won over, they rejected these modifications on the grounds that the resulting guard's cab was now too cramped and the side door let in draughts. The streamlined cars remained in storage until 1950 when they were all converted into ordinary flat ended trailer cars. Sadly as is so often the case, nobody at the time had the foresight, vision or financial muscle to arrange for at least one cab front to be retained for posterity so that we could today admire in the London Transport Museum this bold and confident design solution of 60 years ago.

Front end view of the flat fronted 1935 Stock car showing the skilful retention of the feather grille, the small destination-only window slot, the completely flush fitting access door and the five rectangular headlights.

The interior view looking towards the cab. The end panels after the windows hold upright advertisement frames similar to those on the driver's cab wall. The slope of the floor towards the side doors is particularly apparent.

From the original order for four 6-car trains, the final train was given flat ends, because the streamliners were still a contentious product in several quarters of London Transport. What an inspired solution this was! This revised front end was commendably clean, flush fitting, yet so simple with immaculate proportions and detailing. The manner in which the domed front of the roof was pulled down to an arc which echoed the cab window line has probably never been bettered and the new face of these trains was a dramatic visual improvement over the Standard Stock front ends which instantly appeared crude and archaic by comparison.

The same *feather* shape of the air intake grille was taken from the streamliners but this time was made to accent the form of the domed roof in a particularly satisfactory manner, establishing itself as the all-important key distinguishing feature which all great designs have.

On the final train of 1935 Stock the driving cabs were built with flat ends. This was the true prototype for the classic 1938 Stock and is seen at Northfields Depot in late 1937. The blank panel ahead of the first saloon window was a legacy from the streamlined design and would be replaced by a fourth window on production trains. Though not apparent in this black-and-white photograph, the tops of the cab door and passenger doors were painted grey to match the roof.

BIGGER AND FASTER
TUBE TRAINS

BUT NOT STREAMLINED :
"A FAILURE"

Speedier Tube trains, with a greater seating capacity, have been ordered by London Transport Board following experiments with three types of trains on different lines.

It is hoped with the new trains, writes an *Evening News* representative, to run at least three more an hour on the Morden–Edgware and Bakerloo lines.

It has been decided that the streamlined cars are a failure as far as the Board is concerned. It is most unlikely that we shall ever see any more than the three now in operation on the Piccadilly line.

But it is upon these trains that the Board have based their design for the new stock, and have already ordered 1,050 new tube cars at a cost of more than £6,000,000.

It has been decided that streamlining sacrifices too many passengers for the extra speed, so the new trains will not be stream-lined—although, in the words of a Transport official, "they will have the corners rubbed off."

Evening News report, 12th January 1938.

Left Front end view of a 1938 Stock car.

Absolute perfection!
Side elevation shot taken in October 1938 showing
the domed roof line. The understated elegance and
carefully resolved integrated detailing of the trains'
overall appearance was complemented by the red
livery, with cream window reveals and the gold
London Transport fleet name and car numbers in
LT's own Johnston typeface.

1938 Stock under construction at Metro-Cammell's Birmingham factory.

The 1935 Stock flat-fronted design became the true prototype for the 1938 Stock trains which would eventually result in a massive order of 1121 vehicles shared between Metro-Cammell and Birmingham RCW. Externally the 1938 Stock trains were slightly cleaned up in that the cab front end acquired a larger destination display window area with pleasingly radiused corners, below which were five round headlamp code lights. These replaced the small destination blind and the rectangular lamps from the 1935 trains. The flush-fitting centre cab (or 'M') door featured additional design refinements such as a small glazed panel indicating the train number, rather than having this displayed in the cab window, and a fillet at its base to prevent rain water from entering the cab interior by capillary action. The 1935 flat-fronted trains also had a large blank panel between the first set of double doors and the driver's side door, a legacy from the profiled fronts of the streamlined versions which only allowed three saloon windows in the resulting space. It was therefore an obvious move to install a fourth window and thus the final appearance of 1938 Stock was developed, complemented by the convenience of passenger-operated door open buttons. These were removed in the 1950s because guards often exercised an override switch in service, and consequently caused confusion for the travelling public in knowing whether or not they needed to operate the doors themselves.

The interior design was similarly developed in that the customer unfriendly sharp corners of the draughtscreens from the 1935 trains were replaced by a new design in which the generous radius of the edge of the transverse seats also defined the screen enclosing the longitudinal seat bays (a design concept that was to be repeated on subsequent Underground train interiors for the next 34 years). The profile of these latter draughtscreens was also skilfully opened up to provide a comfortable and convenient hand grip of oval section that both adults and young children could use. Thus, this important safety feature was not only integrated into the form of the draughtscreen, but also provided a consistent visual treatment to the screens throughout the length of the car. An interesting feature which was carried over from London Transport's buses and trolleybuses of the time was that the middle transverse seating units had full length tubular handrails incorporated into the top of the seat back. This feature was never used again on any subsequent tube train design, probably because it could invite children (and tempt certain other passengers) to interfere with the backs of seated travellers. Also, the inner passenger in one of the seats by the draughtscreens, facing a seatback, would have had difficulty in getting out. This was probably the only design fault with these trains; later, two pairs of facing seats in the central section of a tube car would be found to be a much better solution.

The interior design of the very first set of production 1938 Stock vehicles featured generously radiused *user-friendly* corners to the draughtscreens. The seat moquette shown here was designed by Marion Dorn.

Right One of the art deco shovel lamp shades.

Below Bronze ventilation grille detail at car end incorporating car number within bullseye. The light below – situated in the guard's section – illuminated when all the doors were closed.

The beautiful cast glass ribbed shovel-type luminaires in the deco style were, however, carried over from the 1935 series. Their shape allowed the light from their tungsten bulbs to illuminate all parts of the car interior not only very effectively but also with a pleasantly soft and restful ambience. The friendly and agreeable atmosphere that was thus created would be lost in the subsequent vehicles built in the 1960s and '70s, as a result of the harsh light produced by their exposed fluorescent tubes. All of the interior details such as the end of car ventilation grilles and the manner in which the alarm signal stirrup was blended within the ceiling profile were handled with the most careful attention to detail such that this overall excellence was in total harmony with the train's superb exterior design.

The blend of polished wood for the window mullions and other panelling, the 'cerulean blue' paintwork (actually a medium tone of green!), together with the polished chromium plate of the window surrounds for the sliding door pockets and the rich and vibrant moquette designs in red and green, all harmonised magnificently. They created an interior that was welcoming and inviting and at the same time cosy and cosseting. Indeed, it represented the highest point of comfort ever provided for Londoners and it amazed and was the envy of the operators of other metro systems around the world. In the words of Nikolaus Pevsner in his obituary review of Frank Pick's lifetime achievements, in the August 1942 edition of the *Architectural Review*, 'The results of the work on the 1938 tube trains puts the Paris Metro to utter shame and makes the Berlin U-Bahn appear heavy and pedestrian'.

The period of 1935 to 1939 saw the realisation of all Frank Pick's 'patient endeavours,' touching and influencing every aspect of London Transport. These superb new trains, already running in considerable numbers at the outbreak of war, played a major role in achieving a total design excellence wherever one looked. Their backdrop was the excellence of all the new stations designed during the same period by Charles Holden, Stanley Heaps, Reginald Uren, Leonard Bucknell, Herbert Welch and Felix Lander; all influenced and controlled by the unerring eye of Frank Pick himself. 'God is in the details' is the famous quotation by Mies van der Rohe and Londoners now had the opportunity to relish wonderful detailing themselves in every aspect of their journey by London Transport, all of these components harmonising and supporting Pick's grand design to develop the very best urban transport system in the world.

1938 Stock at Piccadilly Circus in the late 1950s in the colour scheme, with dark brown roof and no cream relief, that the trains carried for most of their lives.

Below Integrated design – alarm signal pull down stirrup let into the ceiling profile.

Facing page During the first series build, this final interior effect was achieved whereby the form of the draughtscreen corners was complemented by using a consistent radius for the hooped grab handles and the tubular corners of the transverse seating. This particular seat moquette, featuring the LT bullseye, was designed by Eddie Chapman and made its first appearance during the late 1940s. Partly because these trains were ultimately to be seen on all the tube lines of the London Underground system and carried on in volume to serve Londoners until the late 1970s, they became in time a design icon, representing for travellers the ultimate image of what a tube train looked, sounded and felt like, and following their final departure from serving London in 1988 are still remembered by many with great affection.

SURFACE STOCK TRAINS FOR INNER SUBURBAN AREAS

The period showed similarly outstanding design development of surface vehicles, which culminated in the O, P and Q types which entered service from 1937. As part of the normal depreciation and rolling stock renewal process, 573 cars were ordered from two carbuilders, the Gloucester Railway Carriage & Wagon Company and the Birmingham Railway Carriage & Wagon Company. The last of the deliveries was delayed by the outbreak of the Second World War and was not completed until March 1941. We have seen how the cab front and side elevation of the 1935 M Stock was a development of the stocks built in the 1920s, and they played a role in the development of the O, P and Q Stock trains in that a considerable amount of smoothing, cleaning up and simplification had already taken place. However, O Stock very effectively became the 'big brother' of 1938 Stock. It shared the same clean, elegantly proportioned lines with a closely related cab design with integrated destination panel and headcode lights.

The new order. Photograph taken on 1 September 1937 at Northfields Depot where the first 4-car train of the flare-sided surface trains is on view to the press for the first time. A press release stated that 'The new stock has many advantages over the old. It can be accelerated and braked more quickly, and has air-worked doors as a new feature for the District Line – which can be operated by a button by passengers during non-rush hours. Other features include loose cushions for the seats, new ball-type strap-hangers and various streamlined effects'. This unique photograph shows the train alongside a 1935 streamliner and demonstrates the visual link between the flared treatments on both vehicle types.

The smoothly profiled front of the new generation of surface stock trains. A very effective 'big brother' to the 1938 Tube Stock, with its closely related visual detailing.

One of the main contributing factors creating this sleek appearance was the fact that the generously sized car windows were now flush with the bodyside, effected expensively by the use of rebated glass. The most striking visual feature was the manner in which the body sides flared out at the bottom, and the lower end of the sliding doors also followed this contour. Thus the flared front of the 1935 streamlined cars was somehow reinstated but now on the sides! This feature gave the cars an exceptionally pleasing appearance but it also had three important functional purposes. It assisted the mechanical cleaning of the trains, replaced the side running boards that were provided on earlier stocks and filled in the gap between train and platform.

In the days of manually operated doors on surface stock trains, the highly dangerous practice would sometimes occur where a passenger would make a run for a train just as it was leaving a station, aim for the running board and then hang onto the outside! This was particularly prevalent in hot weather when the doors were sometimes left partially or fully open. With the old hand-worked sliding doors, there was always a vertical handrail both outside and inside at each door leaf. These were provided for passengers to hold on to when opening the doors, for they were quite heavy to open or shut. Thus these handrails made it simple to ride on the outside and it was rightfully considered that such temptations had to be designed out of the new stock. On the older train types, they ultimately were all to go with conversion to air door operation.

This photograph of an O Stock 2-car unit shows off well the flared sides, the similar manner in which both the double and single passenger doors were skilfully recessed into the body sides and the chamfered form of the glazing on top of the windows.

The manner in which both single and double sliding doors were recessed into the body sides was also similar to 1938 Stock as was the incorporation of the same design of door open button. Another characteristic appearance feature of these trains was the chamfered shape of the glazing panels at the top of the windows which prevented rain entering the ventilation panels when they were opened.

The family resemblance to 1938 Tube Stock was also followed through to the interior design, except that the draughtscreen design, with the detailing of their vertical grabpoles, was directly inherited from the previous 1931/35 builds of surface stock. The same colour of cerulean blue (mid-green) was also used and the various varnished wood panels and trims featured inlaid ebonised wood (the workmanship of which being to the highest standards of marquetry). The lessons learned from

illuminating the ceiling profile on the 1935 and 1938 Tube Stocks were however carried across with the same shovel type luminaires illuminating essentially the same elliptical section of painted ceiling panels. In order to keep cleaning easy, most of the internal right angles were filled with a fillet – for instance between floor and seat risers etc. The line containing the fixings for the strap hangers was another feature where there was now a close visual relationship between both sizes of stock. All of the train types featured deeply upholstered seats for maximum passenger comfort, but only the transverse seating fitted to O Stock motor cars had high backs extending above the window line, which was a historical throwback to the previous types of surface stock interiors. These seats were originally fitted with semi-loose cushions covered with moquette which gave the characteristic deep buttoned appearance seen

Above Interior of an O Stock motor car when new. Although the ceiling profile and the shovel lamps are carried over from the 1935/38 Stock tube designs, the tubular ends of the grabpoles were inherited from previous designs of surface stock. Note the chamfered bases of the transverse seats to facilitate cleaning – only O Stock driving cars had high backs fitted to these seats, which extended above the window base line. The two close fitting panes of glass that were located in the centre bay positions to direct cooling air down to the metadyne unit can just be seen.

Facing page The O and P Stock trailer cars and all builds of the P and Q Stock featured transverse seating with back tops aligning with lower window frames.

in the photographs, but these were later converted to the standard type of interior sprung seats fitted to subsequent stock types. Those illustrated above in an original car are trimmed with another design by Enid Marx called Brent which was also new. Transverse seat back tops of the O and P Stock trailer cars and all of the P and Q Stock type builds were all lower and aligned with the lower edge of window frames.

The O Stock motor cars were fitted with a new system of electrical control which had been developed by Metropolitan Vickers, known as the Metadyne system. This involved the provision of a rotary transformer placed between the line supply and the traction motors. The fitting of this equipment impacted on the interior design of cars in that partitions in the centre bays had two panes of glass, with space between to channel clean air from the saloon to cool the Metadyne unit and these can just be discerned in the photograph. On P Stock the required cooling air would be directed via an intake under the middle companion seats. First Class compartments were also offered on these trains and illustrated on pages 74 and 75 is a P Stock trailer car showing such a compartment. Standard fare travellers sat on seats covered in a plainer moquette – it was presumably considered that passengers were getting more for their money by sitting on Bushey fabric, also designed by Enid Marx! The First Class facility was withdrawn at the outbreak of the Second World War and was never reinstated.

Left The interior of one of the new trailer cars photographed in 1938 showing the closed off First Class compartment that was located between doored partitions. In this case, Enid Marx's *Bushey* moquette pattern provided the more expensive seating environment. First Class sections such as these would soon disappear with the outbreak of the Second World War, but the tell-tale inner door framing would stay in position until the end of their lives.

Above left and right
Posed shot of door being operated by passenger (who would have been a member of the staff) and showing the convenience of the new strap hangers.

Experiments were made with door interlock lights to provide an indication to the guard of doors not fully closed. These would be incorporated into the postwar builds of the similar R Stock which followed.

CHAPTER FOUR

The years 1945 to 1966

SURFACE STOCK TRAINS

DISTRICT LINE

The first new fleet of surface stock trains to be delivered after the Second World War was the R Stock, built to replace the old hand-operated door stocks still working on the Circle and District Lines. These trains were virtually identical to the pre-war O and P types and the first batch (classified R47) was delivered in 1949 with red painted steel bodies. It was then decided that the second batch (R49) would have bodies and underframes built of corrosion resistant aluminium alloy. Though the change quickly came to be seen as a weight-saving (and therefore power-saving) measure, the early post-war shortage of steel was the initial impulse for using aluminium. It was to prove

This LONDON TRANSPORT car was selected by the Council of Industrial Design as an exhibit in the South Bank Exhibition of the Festival of Britain May-September 1951

LIGHTWEIGHT ROLLING STOCK

successful and all Underground rolling stock since 1953 has been built with aluminium bodywork. It was estimated that leaving the cars unpainted would save two tons per eight car train in addition to the 5.4 ton per car (12½ per cent) reduction in weight resulting in changing from steel to aluminium alloy. One car of R49 Stock was thus left unpainted from this first order and a complete unpainted train followed later. All other R49 Stock was red on delivery. One of the aluminium vehicles, part painted red and part unpainted, was featured in the Transportation Pavilion of the 1951 Festival of Britain exhibition at London's South Bank. This was LT's own statement of the post-war 'swords to ploughshares' philosophy where the advanced technology that had been developed during the war was now being directed to new peacetime uses. The first eight car, all aluminium unpainted train went into passenger service at the beginning of 1953 and its uncompromising metallic appearance was relieved by the application of a red horizontal band. Thirteen new cars were ordered in 1959, also in unpainted alloy.

Externally there were slight changes from the pre-war O and P stock design in that a roller blind destination display now replaced the enamel plates that were fitted behind a display panel; this was located above the non-driving cab window. As far as their interior design was concerned, the same expensive pre-war style of inlaid ebonised wood was still used to decorate the wooden seat backs and the inner faces of the draughtscreens during that austere and bleak post-war period. Transverse seats in which the back tops aligned with the window base line (from P Stock) were continued, but a post-war refinement was introduced. The previous dead space created by the solid panelling below the windows was exploited to create more elbow

'SILVER' TRAIN IS A NO-PAINT TEST

THE first "silver train" on the Underground came into service on the District Line in the rush-hour to-day.

The exterior is unpainted bright aluminium alloy instead of London Transport's traditional red. It is an economy experiment to see if light-weight aluminium alloy can be left unpainted in London Underground conditions.

A complete new train requires two tons of paint initially and over 5cwt. when repainted at periodical overhaul.

Facing page The post-war all-aluminium R Stock vehicles were hailed as being a world first. Car 23231 was proudly displayed in the Transportation Pavilion at the 1951 Festival of Britain. The photograph shows it on its trailer being manoeuvred into position outside that building.

Facing page inset Enamel plaque inside car 23231.

Above The entry into service of the first unpainted train as reported in the *Evening News* of Monday 19 January 1953.

An interior view of these post-war trains, fitted with fluorescent lighting and sporting the then ubiquitous *bullseye* moquette designed by Eddie Chapman, however still with the marquetry and ebonised timber inlay on the backs of both the transverse seats and the inner faces of draughtscreens. The 'fit for purpose' chamfered detail on the base of these seats to facilitate cleaning was naturally carried over from the pre-war vehicles, but there was now an additional skilful touch to further aid cleaning and also to improve passenger comfort. The hollowed-out window panel was designed to achieve greater elbow room. Note also the neat interface between the radiused corner of this panel and the trimmed edge of the moquette.

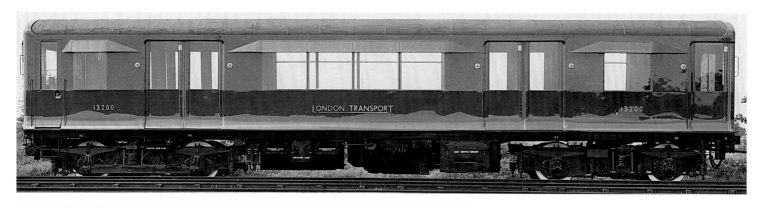

Above Comparison of 1938 P Stock and 1953 R Stock cars. On the latter the mid-car windows were fewer and larger and their ventilators of an improved design. Note how the car number was neatly incorporated onto the red band. The difference in door spacing reflects the fact that O and P Stocks were intended to run in 2-car units which meant that there were two cab to cab portions in the body of a train. This fact resulted in the double doors being positioned nearer to the cab ends in order to provide even door spacing throughout a train's length. In contrast an R Stock 6-car train only had cabs at the extreme ends; thus the doors no longer needed to be near them and so they were brought closer together on driving motor cars.

An early photograph of the first unpainted aluminium car taken in service in June 1952.

room for passengers. This was effected by scooping out these panels and blending the trimmed edge of the moquette by a neat interface detail. Thus, not only passenger comfort but also cleanability was greatly improved; just what good design is all about! The previously specified cast glass shovel tungsten bulb luminaires were now replaced by bare two-foot fluorescent tubes; this was the first time that any production Underground train had been fitted throughout with such lighting. These were successfully integrated into the overall design and, as a result, did not appear to be stuck on as an afterthought, as were the first installations on tube stock.

Left and below The red banding on the first complete train of unpainted aluminium stock was carried in a horizontal line across the front. However 'Joe' Manser, who had succeeded William Graff-Baker as Chief Mechanical Engineer is on record as wanting something more dynamic in appearance, and so the frontal treatment was soon changed. The angle and tapering thickness of the revised 'V' shaped band was skilfully contrived to just clear the bottom left hand corner of the train number display and the top right hand indicator lamp.

Left At the beginning of the 1960s there was considerable international interest still being shown in these trailblazing aluminium cars. One of the unpainted cars from the 1959 batch of trailers is being loaded onto a ferry for outward transportation to the International Aluminium Exhibition held at Strasbourg in 1960. Passenger door control was not in use when these cars were delivered.

The story of London Underground's unique moquette patterns

1923 – Lozenge, Anon

1929 – Art deco pattern, Isaac Jennings

1936 – Belsize, Enid Marx

1937 – Caledonian, Marion Dorn

1937 – Brent, Enid Marx

1938 – Chevron, Enid Marx

We have seen how seats covered in patterned cut-pile wool moquette have been a feature of London Underground's trains since the early 1920s. This tradition has been maintained to the present day and such seating has over the years become an intrinsic part of the unique character of these trains. Indeed these deeply upholstered seats that are fully compliant to the human form are what everyone expects to sit in when they ride on London's Underground trains; they are a fundamental part of the culture and experience of travelling underneath and around the capital by

Historical design review

In the past, train upholstery whether used on London's underground trains or those belonging to the main line steam railway companies had mimicked the styles common in the home. In the twenties and early to mid thirties, the popular vogue for floral and 'art deco' inspired styles were echoed on all of these trains, using the same colour palettes used in home furnishings. Experience had shown the most hardwearing material for transport seating was moquette, a material woven on special Jaquard looms by only a few firms. This is a very durable material which has the greatest capacity for absorbing the impact of body pressure. Moquette has naturally only a small number of customers but is usually bought in large quantities. Up to this time, there had not been sufficient demand or competition to stimulate experiments with design or to develop patterns that were contemporary and unique.

Lozenge, the first moquette fabric to be designed specifically for use on both London's underground and overground rolling stock in the 1920s that was also standardised for use on other vehicles owned by the Underground Group such as its buses, tramcars and trolleybuses has already been described. It was produced by Firth's Furnishings Ltd in Yorkshire, and its small motif enabled economies to be made in cutting and pattern matching. Its use marked a departure in design, and it remained in service into the 1930s; being manufactured by a further two companies, Lister & Co. of Bradford and John Holdsworth & Co. of Halifax. The latter company still produces the majority of London Underground's requirements even today. They have very kindly rewoven, especially for this book, some of the most famous and striking historical patterns ever used on Underground trains and these are an interesting feature of this work.

The fabric designs that were to revolutionise the interior of London Underground trains originated in 1936 when Christian Barman, the Publicity Officer of the then London Passenger Transport Board, wanted to commission some new fabric designs for the new generation of tube trains which were to become known as the 1938 Tube Stock.

Barman had been directly appointed by Frank Pick and they both approached freelance, rather than in-house designers to create customised fabrics that were worthy of the modern age. Enid Marx was the first of four designers approached; the others were Marion Dorn, Norbert Dutton and Paul Nash. Their particular success in the task was both a reflection of their talent and the ability of Barman to convey his requirements.

The original brief was highly

electric train. It would be unacceptable to the passengers of these trains to consider exchanging such seats with other types that are accepted by the users of other Metro systems around the world. Moulded phenolic plastic seats with padded inserts that are used in Paris, Berlin and Vienna would not be tolerated by London's commuters and even less so would be the stainless steel seating of the Hong Kong trains! Furthermore, since most of the trains are stabled overnight in the open, seats in these latter materials would be particularly unwelcoming in winter months!

specific. The fabrics had to be hard wearing and not show dirt; furthermore the patterns and colours had to be pleasing in both natural and artificial light and not create 'dazzle' when in motion. It was suggested that the new patterns should be seen as a symbol of the Underground's unification of the country and the city.

1945 – Shield, Enid Marx

1947 – Roundel, Eddie Chapman

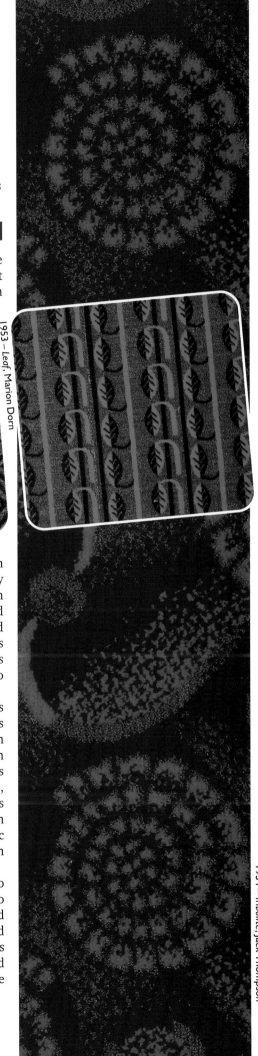

1953 – Leaf, Marion Dorn

1954 – Tribolite, Jack Thompson

In Enid Marx's own words, the textiles "had to look fresh under pretty awful conditions. As the trains were used by all classes and trades going to and from work, sometimes in greasy overalls, dirt stains were inevitable. Short journeys and rush hour traffic produced heavy wear and tear, to which some parts of the seats and backs were more exposed than others". She was not in favour of using floral designs in the trains, due to their association with the home. The sizes and different shapes of the seats meant that the pattern repeats should not be too large (she adhered to the original specification of a 12½inch repeat, or multiples thereof).

Her first design was called *Belsize*, this cut pile moquette was sampled by Messrs Holdsworth & Co. in 1936. It was a bold and simple geometric weave that was developed to solve the problem of 'dazzle'. *Brent* was her next pattern, produced in 1937 and *Chevron* followed in 1938. This continued to be used after the war when trains on two lines were re-upholstered in 1949. Possibly her most famous pattern was *Shield*; first manufactured by Holdsworth's in 1945 which was used for the Bakerloo, Northern and District Lines. *Roundel*, incorporating the LT bar and circle device was designed by Eddie Chapman in 1947 and perhaps Marion Dorn's most pleasing design was her *Leaf* motif; also produced in red and green which was a softer, less geometric design. This pattern went through many permutations and the definitive design illustrated was first produced in 1953.

These patterns had a varied life span and several were still a familiar sight to passengers at the end of the 1950s. Jack Thompson's *Tribolite* was the last design to retain the spirit of that distinctive approach which had characterised Underground train interiors for 25 years and therefore was the final legacy of the initiatives created by both Pick and Barman The moquettes developed from the early 1960s onwards were plainer and more perfunctory in style and lacked the individuality and uniqueness of their predecessors. This philosophy was not to change until the refurbishment era commenced in the late 1980s.

MODERNISING THE MET

At the end of the war, there was a need to order new trains not only to coincide with the electrification of the Metropolitan Line from Rickmansworth to Amersham and Chesham, but also to replace those trains that were composed of teak bodied compartment coaches; either electric locomotive hauled or T Stock multiple units. These were now to be replaced by saloon cars with air operated doors, fewer seats and more standing accommodation, but the most important factor was the requirement to provide through car gangways so that passengers could be speedily evacuated from trains, particularly in tunnel sections. Before the A Stock with its through gangways, the single bore tunnel sections on the line had emergency walkways built into them alongside the trains.

Just before the war started in September 1939, two unusual mock-ups had been built at Acton Works to investigate the possibility of retaining individually walled-off transverse seating compartments with their own set of air controlled sliding doors in a car that would also have a full length corridor. The photographs below and opposite show a somewhat bizarre solution where the doors also double as windows and would have opened for only half their length. Adjacent doors, such as those either side of the 'London Transport' lettering, would have overlapped in the door pocket. It is interesting to note that both door closing, as well as door opening buttons, were suggested for passenger use, certainly ahead of their time.

A mock-up built in 1939 at Acton Works showing a compartment type configuration for the seating but with air operated doors. The doors would have doubled as windows and would have opened for half their width. Adjacent doors, such as those either side of the London Transport fleetname, would have overlapped the door pocket. Door closing, as well as door opening buttons, were on offer for passengers, no doubt because doors left open unnecessarily would have to be avoided.

Left The interior view. Each car would have had eight compartments.

Below Another mock-up built at about the same time showing a less complicated arrangement for air door operated compartment stock. Again, the doors would have opened for only half their width.

The first interior mock-up of the proposed Amersham Line Stock which was completed in August 1944. Note the first innovative application of fluorescent tube lighting; the seats were trimmed with Marion Dorn's *Caledonian* moquette. With the sofa seating positioned adjacent to the sliding doors, clearly no one was thinking about the effect of winter weather with driving horizontal rain and snow!

Another view of the mock-up produced at Acton in August 1944 for Amersham Stock.

As the war drew to a close further thoughts of what these trains might look like were already in the minds of some engineers based at Acton Works and a mock-up was constructed in August 1944 for 'Amersham Line Stock'. It included the very first application of fluorescent lighting within a London Transport rail vehicle. These ideas were then developed into a prototype car 17000 which was built with two side corridors and island seating arranged in sets of three and ran in service in this form for three years from the beginning of 1946. Not surprisingly this arrangement proved to be very unpopular with passengers because the layout provided hardly any window seats. These island seats meant that passengers were completely cut off from the windows when both corridors were filled with standing passengers.

Interior of the prototype Amersham Line Stock trailer car 17000 which was completed at the end of 1945. This embodied the ideas from the wartime mock-up. Although arm rests were not provided, the seats were shaped to define the seating position.

Right A view of the passenger accommodation. Both leaves of all doors could be opened and closed by the guard, but passengers could also open or close one leaf of each pair.

Below right Plan of seating and door arrangements.

Below A portion of the interior seen through the open doors – very chilly for passengers during the savage winter conditions of 1947, the worst on record.

Bottom The complete car in original state.

This prototype was then modified (and renumbered to 17001) such that the side corridors were replaced by a middle gangway with three passenger seats on one side and two on the other. This layout must have performed very satisfactorily in service as it eventually became the model for the new A Stock trains that were delivered from 1960 to 1962 whose general interior design closely followed it.

A second prototype car, numbered 20000, entered service in June 1947 and ran as a pair with 17000. It seated 56 passengers all in pairs, with a central gangway. The seats had recessed armrests and moulded back squabs. Continuous luggage racks were fitted and flourescent lighting was again used. Both of these cars were finally scrapped in 1955, having served their purpose as rolling test beds in connection with the design work for the replacement Metropolitan rolling stock.

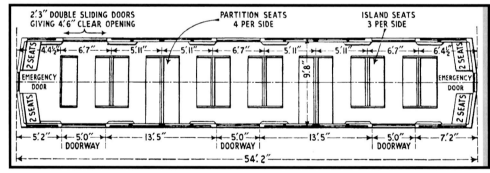

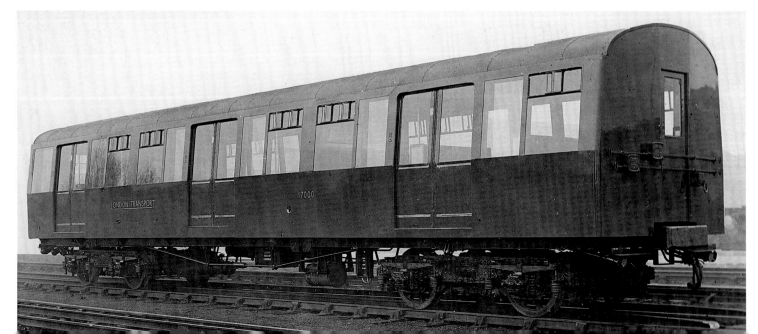

Top Car 20000 and car 17000 in a train formation outside Acton Works.

Above Testing the door opening and closing buttons.

Above left Due to the unpopularity of the layout, car 17000 was completely refitted three years later with a modified seating layout of three seats one side and two on the other side of an off-centre gangway. The seats were trimmed in Shield, an Enid Marx design first produced by Holdsworth in 1945. As can be seen, some of the seats were provided with high backs and others with low ones. Renumbered 17001 this car entered service at the end of 1949.

Below left The interior of the second prototype car 20000 with two-plus-two seating, which entered service in June 1947. The advertising panel reads: '. . . the interior has been designed to meet the varying needs of two distinct services: a country service to Amersham and a town service between Finchley Road and the City'.

The exterior of a later 'Amersham car' mock-up which was built at Acton Works in early 1950. In styling terms it was to be very much the 'big brother' of the proposed 1952 Tube Stock (see pages 102–5), with the same sharp edge design, similar shape and proportions to the cab windows, running lights, car number and ventilation grilles.

In the middle of 1950, another mock-up for the new electrified Metropolitan Line stock was built at Acton Works, but was soon discarded because electrification was again postponed. It bore a marked similarity to the abandoned 1952 Tube Stock proposals both in terms of its exterior styling and also the use of similar circular windows in the door pocket positions. The same off-centre gangway with three-plus-two seating was again employed. Towards the end of the 1950s, with all of the lessons learnt from these various mock-ups, London Transport's engineers had finally consolidated their thoughts and ideas for what the new Amersham Stock should look like. One last development interior mock-up was built in 1958 to demonstrate the final design of the high backed seating that was being planned.

Two views of the 1950 mock-up interior design. Circular windows in the door pockets, similar to the 1949 sunshine tube car, were proposed and the seating layout reverted to three plus two either side of an off-centre gangway. The deep transverse bulkheads with their line diagrams would become a feature of the eventual new A Stock, which remains to this day. The luggage racks fitted above the seats would become a familiar feature of the contemporary slam-door stock then being built for British Railways, but these never had LT's proposed dividing panels which ensured that cases and other articles could not be removed by the adjacent passengers!

In 1959 an order was placed with Cravens of Sheffield for 248 cars which were to replace the teak bodied T Stock and the locomotive hauled steam stock following the extension of the electrified tracks from Rickmansworth to Amersham, including the branch to Chesham. A further order would be placed for 216 similar cars to enable the service to Uxbridge to be provided by the same stock; thus allowing the old oval front window F Stock trains of 1920 to be finally withdrawn.

The external styling of the production cars strongly echoed that of experimental car 20000 with the same crease-line running below the window line and crisply detailed windows. The cab was pleasingly detailed with satisfying proportions and the trains retained the traditional family relationship with contemporary tube trains.

The original interior detailing of these cars was solidly yet neatly executed and fibreglass mouldings featured for the first time in their construction. The seat backs were moulded in this material and their form extended up to the ceiling area to provide transverse locations for the line diagrams. Glass was incorporated in these mouldings to form the draught screens for every door vestibule. Plastic laminates were used for all the end wall and window surround facings and profiled timber coving pieces were fitted to facilitate cleaning. The metal heater covers in the seat bases were shaped to give maximum strength allied to pleasing appearance. Bare 4ft fluorescent lighting tubes were fitted in all cars and individual satin anodised luggage racks were fitted throughout. The colour scheme was an unremitting grey, which was however pleasingly highlighted by maroon facings on the car ends. The moquette pattern was an effective but undistinguished design in grey, red and black.

Externally, high quality light alloy castings were left in natural finish and they skilfully shaped all the required transitional forms of the carbody. These complemented the exterior panelling of unpainted alloy sheet. Body exteriors of A Stock were made up of three types of aluminium – cast, extruded and sheet. Because of the different methods of production, they were not all of the same colour and had different textures. The overall effect, therefore, was one of a slight patchwork. By the end of the 1980s the trains were looking particularly careworn and even hostile as a result of the grafitti epidemic that was particularly prevalent on the Met at the time. The refurbishment programme would come just in time to give them a very effective new lease of life in passenger service.

Facing page above Getting there. Yet another partial interior mock-up that was built in 1958 and which was now defining the final appearance. The individual aluminium luggage racks would be a feature of the production trains and, for cost reasons, would survive in the refurbished vehicles still in service at the time of writing.

Facing page below Interior of brand new A60 Stock driving car viewed from the guard's position. The seat moquette was a new design also used on contemporary 1959 and 1962 tube stocks.

Above A scale model undergoing strain gauge tests in Cravens' engineering department.

Right The side of an
A Stock car during
construction and before
fixing to its underframe.

Below Six cars at a later
stage of build in
Cravens' works.

Above Exterior view of a 1961 A Stock train as originally delivered. They are formed from cars built with particularly sturdy construction methods, and although developed from a design now half a century old, continue to provide (albeit in substantially refurbished form, see later chapter) all the Metropolitan Line services. They are still capable of impressive speeds away from the central area; however the quality of ride certainly leaves a lot to be desired.

Left Interior view of a 1961 A Stock train as originally delivered.

Right In 1949, ventilation fans were fitted experimentally to a train of 1938 Stock; facilities for fans were also provided on R Stock but were never fitted. The proposal was not adopted at the time and would have to wait a further 24 years before being introduced on 1973 Tube Stock.

Facing page The large standback spaces incorporating perch seats that were fitted experimentally to a 1938 Stock trailer car in 1956. They stayed in position until the car was eventually scrapped in 1977. They opened up a much wider standing area near the doors where it was most needed and were the true forerunner of the standback spaces which would later become such an important feature for passengers in crowded trains. The concept of a padded 'perch seat' in this position would eventually re-appear in the mid-1990s on new and refurbished tube trains.

Facing page inset Photograph showing the L-shaped perch seat being used; presumably posed by LT staff members. The body language shows that the seat's potential to develop a friendly conversation between the two of them has, on this occasion, failed miserably!

TUBE STOCK TRAINS

As far as London Underground was concerned, the post-war period started with the delivery in 1946 of the balance of the build order for the 1938 Tube Stock. In 1949 there was a further order of 70 uncoupling non-driving motor cars and 21 trailer cars. The development of the 70 UNDMs was significant in that the contents of a driving cab were fitted into the space of a 'cupboard'. The spin-offs were considerable – not just the usually trumpeted advantage of lower cost but the more subtle benefits of increased passenger space and, most important of all, the breaking up of a thirty-five foot absence of passenger door access right in the middle of a train which was a serious inconvenience caused by driving cabs. Another feature of 1949 Stock was the redesign of the communication door windows which finally eliminated the time-honoured leather adjustment strap. The spring loaded latch system that replaced it has been used ever since. These trains, together with their duly modified 1935 counterparts and the rest of the 1938 Stock fleet then continued to serve London for several decades.

During the service life of 1938 Stock, a number of interesting modifications were carried out and tried in service and whilst some of them were not taken up at the time for fleet use, many of them live on in the trains of today. Examples of these are:
1.	Circular ceiling fan housings were fitted in 1949 into a 1938 Stock car and one complete train.

2.   Fluorescent light fittings were being used in the new post-war stations being built, particularly both the eastern and western extensions of the Central Line and their appropriateness was also investigated in tube and surface stock cars.

3.   An interesting experiment fitted to a 1938 Stock trailer car in 1956 was an attempt to solve the problem of passengers blocking doorways. This was (and remains today on some designs) a problem in rush hour traffic and a large standback space with perch seats was fitted to overcome it. This treatment, however, remained a one-off but the vehicle remained in service until 1977 when it was scrapped. As we will later see, this idea was resurrected after a period of some 35 years to be used again in tube trains.

The end of the war saw Britain's entire railway system in an extremely run down condition with shortages of materials, fuel and staff exacerbated by the results of

Facing page above From the passengers' perspective! Photograph taken in December 1949 to accompany a press release which ran: "Heather Thatcher, the popular *Linda* of the *Family Affairs* television show, went for a trip on the new *sunshine roof* coach of the London Passenger Transport Board on the Bakerloo Line this morning." Many customs have changed since then, not least, the number of staff available to see her off!

Facing page below The revised external appearance of what became known as the *sunshine car*.

Below The partial conversion to provide windows extending into the roof which was shown to Lord Latham in mid-1949. He then approved the conversion of a whole car which was completed in the late autumn of the same year. Note the detail differences between this and the completed car 10306.

On the elevation of Lord Ashfield to head the newly formed British Transport Commission, Lord Latham, who had been an LPTB member since 1937 and leader of the London County Council, left to become chairman of the London Transport Executive on 1st January 1948.

enemy action and deferred maintenance. The grand scheme for the expansion of the Underground system known as the 1935–1940 New Works Programme, which was in full swing in summer 1939, had, of course, completely ground to a halt during the war. London Transport was not able to get Government financial backing for all the projects in this programme; the economic austerity of those years saw to that and in any case, the needs of the badly run down British Railways network took precedence. LT was now just a cog in the wheel of the newly nationalised British Transport Commission. Thus these immense post-war difficulties made a full scale reinstatement of the work impossible, but plans were drawn up for a partial resumption of the programme with the extensions to the west and east of the Central Line given the greatest priority.

The rolling stock originally earmarked for these extensions consisted of Standard Stock cars dating from 1923 to 1927 which had been stored in the open throughout the war and as a result were in very poor condition. A total of 340 cars were stripped down and completely rebuilt between 1946 and 1948. Due to the war, the Piccadilly Line had never received its promised ten extra trains that were part of the original New Works Programme and so part of the reinstated plan was to order 100 brand new seven car trains for this line to replace its own fleet of Standard Stock cars. The best of these older trains would then be cascaded onto the extended Central to provide 8-car trains, with the oldest ones of them being scrapped. It was intended that the new trains would be to the same basic design as the 1938 Tube Stock but known as the 1951 Stock, their planned date of introduction, and a number of technical improvements were proposed as well as some key ones affecting their appearance.

Mr W S Graff-Baker was still very much in evidence as Chief Mechanical Engineer and he rightly held the view that standing passengers inside tightly packed tube cars were handicapped by the fact that they could not see the station names unless they stooped to look through the windows (this problem remains today in the passenger saloon areas of most tube stocks). His solution was to raise the height of the windows, and the restricted height of the tube car body meant that this glazing had to extend into the curved roof line. As part of the early design work being carried out for future tube stock, an experiment was carried out in 1949 to provide these larger windows. It was hoped to introduce them on the planned 1951 Tube Stock.

Pages overleaf The striking improvements gained in both lightness and airiness that resulted from the *vista-car* design approach.

Above View of *sunshine car* from the driving end.

Below The Underground still held a fascination with schoolboys even after five years of war when they had been starved of their hobby and submitted instead to newer mechanical inventions. The *Eagle* was published weekly for the more inquisitive boy and ran this centre spread showing the guts of a tube train which included the latest experimental car body.

A partial conversion was shown in 1949 to the Chairman of London Transport, Lord Latham, who approved the remodelling of a whole car that was completed in November of the same year. The car was suitably modified such that the windows in each door and the centre pair of windows between the doorways were extended up into the roof. The door pocket windows were replaced by circular 'portholes' which though a simple and stylish solution, nevertheless ironically gave even less outward visibility for some passengers!

This vehicle, known as the vista car or sunshine car, remained in service for nearly thirty years, being finally unceremoniously scrapped in 1980. This was another unfortunate example of a key development in the evolving design history of Underground cars not being recognised in time. Two drawings were produced for the planned 1952 Tube Stock (the design had slipped back a year), one very much as the prototype vista car and the other maintaining square windows either side of the doors together with additional horizontal glazing bars on the doors aligning with them.

A fully finished mock-up was produced at Acton Works to define this new design

which proposed fluorescent tubes and fan cowlings in the ceiling. Externally, the destination panel was located above the driver's entrance door which interestingly was a return to where it had been positioned on the earliest 1923 Standard Stock cars. In visual design terms this would mean sacrificing the beautifully sculpted domed roof front of 1938 Stock. Some odd styling details were also now creeping in which were at odds with the purity of the 1938 Stock's overall shape. These were a soft barrelling to the body sides which led into a sharp transition at cantrail level and a distinctly sharp edged treatment around the edge of the cab. Also apparent is that the face of the cab was slightly bowed in both directions. It could be the case that these latter details were influenced by the then current styling vogue for razor edged motor cars in Britain such as the Triumph Renown and Mayflower.

A new type of bogie was also produced for the 1952 Stock. It incorporated the use of rubber instead of steel springs for both primary and secondary suspension units and although some experiments in the use of rubber suspension had taken place on a District Line car, this was a more advanced version. There were also significant changes in car body construction proposed for these trains, in that the bodywork above floor level was to be manufactured from aluminium instead of steel. Calculations revealed that a weight saving of only 12 per cent was possible because the complex nature of the car underframe demanded that it had still to be built from steel. Metro-Cammell was given a contract to carry out design work on the 'high-window car' and they and other manufacturers were also asked to submit tenders for a 700 car order based on the 1938 Stock design either in steel or aluminium. By mid-1951, various manufacturers were quoting a cost of an additional 15 per cent for an aluminium bodied car compared to the traditional steel one. A saving of energy and other operating costs against this was proved over a 30-year life, but it was only marginal. Interestingly the maintenance savings that could be achieved by never having to paint the trains during their life was not part of the equation!

For the new 1952 Stock it was unfortunately decided to abandon the high window concept because of the uncertainty of their costs when compared to the conventional design (they were quoted as being between £110 and £350 extra per car at 1951 prices). An interesting design debate then ensued. Alec Valentine, one of the board members, suggested that keeping the high windows in the doors only would not involve the expensive body structure redesign of the original and would clearly be of benefit to the majority of standing passengers packed in the door vestibules. Mr A W Manser, known as Joe Manser, then Graff-Baker's deputy, persuaded him that such a scheme would "spoil the side elevation" of a new train.

Two coloured drawings prepared at Acton Works showing possible designs for 1952 Tube Stock. Both still draw heavily on 1938 Tube Stock; the lower version shows windows extended into the roof line but with additional framing to the door glazing to reduce costs. These gave a dated, pedestrian appearance to the car's side elevation. In contrast the first illustration is similar to the stylish *vista car*.

A W (Joe) Manser, then Graff-Baker's deputy.

Sir Alec Valentine, Board member from 1948 and Chairman of London Transport from 1959 to 1965.

Below Mock-up of the bogie with rubber suspension that was proposed for the 1952 Stock. In the event, the bogies that would be used on what would eventually be called 1956–62 Stock were more like 1949 stock bogies adapted to rubber – particularly the primary suspension.

Below and right The fully finished mock-up produced at Acton Works in 1952 of the planned 1952 Stock design. This incorporated the roof glazing ideas taken from the prototype *sunshine car*, but the elegant curvature of the original was now replaced by a sharper, more faceted treatment using flat glass in order to reduce costs. Fluorescent lighting and ceiling fans were also incorporated. The ceiling mounted square light was intended for emergencies.

Bottom The double doorway of the proposed stock showing the extended glazing created by the two flat panels with support framing. Passenger door controls were mounted on thin door pillars.

Later, Alec Valentine was knighted. He had served London Transport and its predecessors since 1928 and became Chairman of London Transport from 1959 to 1965 during the period when the new Victoria Line was being developed. He resurrected and strongly promoted this feature and instructed that it must be incorporated into the new trains for this line. Joe Manser had also in the meantime become the LT Board's Chief Mechanical Engineer and held this post when the line was opened in 1969. High windows in tube train doors have since been specified on every new tube train design built. This is a good example of the axiom that where matters of design are concerned, the ideas that usually succeed into production are those which are owned by, and are personal to, people who have the power and authority to force them through.

The whole programme then started to drift again. Deliveries of other train types, such as the aforementioned 1949 Tube Stock, and the sudden death of William Graff-Baker, who had tragically collapsed in the street outside his home in Kensington in 1952, were the main reasons, but the organisation was still stretched by the national economic crisis then prevailing as well as the continuing shortages of energy and materials.

We have already seen how the tremendous energy, vision, and strength of purpose of just a handful of strong and powerful personalities had shaped the London Transport system over the years. An unprecedented era of major innovation in rolling stock design also died with the passing of Graff-Baker and it would take another 30 years before we would again see a major rebirth in resolving technical and design issues in a similar totally innovatory fashion.

Two views of the external styling for the proposed stock. Note the sharp crease line at cantrail level, taken from the intersection point of the two panels of flat glass, to achieve glazing into the roof profile. The softly barrelled shape applied to the lower body side (echoes of the UCC built Standard Stock cars) and the sharp cab corners are also clearly visible. The destination indicator returns to its original position above the cab door, last seen in 1923 on tube trains.

Below Could the razor-edged appearance of this contemporary Triumph *Renown* car have been a styling influence?

William Graff-Baker

B.Sc.(Eng.) A.C.G.I., M.I.Mech.E, M.I.Loco.E, M.Inst.T.,
and Member of the American Society of Mechanical Engineers

An appreciation

October, 1937

THE RAILWAY MAGAZINE

New London Underground Stock

THE new cars now being placed in service for the Metropolitan and District Lines of the London Passenger Transport Board incorporate many notable refinements. They are semi-permanently coupled together into two-car units, the outer ends having automatic couplers electro-pneumatically controlled by push buttons in the driver's cab. These couplers complete mechanical and pneumatic connections, but not electrical. Each car is 51 ft. 1¼ in. long and has seating for 40 passengers. The doors are pneumatically worked and, at busy times will be opened and closed by the guard as on a tube train, but during slack hours each door may be opened from inside or outside by press-button control by passengers. Internally the cars are similar to the latest stock, with loose-cushion seats, cheerful colouring and bright lighting. The new stock can be accelerated and braked very much more quickly than the present stock. Whereas the latter can be accelerated at 1 to 1.2 m.p.h. per sec., the new stock can pick up speed at 2 m.p.h. per sec. The braking speed of the new stock is 3 m.p.h. per sec., and a train of eight cars travelling at 40 m.p.h. can be pulled up dead in 500 ft., or practically its own length. These improvements have been made possible by the use of the metadyne system of controlling the supply of current to the traction motors which permits of regenerative braking. An ingenious new feature is that the metadyne draws the air it requires for self-cooling from inside the car in such a way as to provide forced ventilation. To separate the smoking from the non-smoking sections of the car double glass panels are used between the seat backs, and air is sucked by the metadyne through the space between the glass panels; thus tobacco smoke is immediately drawn out of the car. The bogies are of all-welded construction, and the 36-in. wheels are mounted on roller bearings. The bogie centres also have roller bearings. Each 2-car unit which weighs 71½ tons is driven by four traction motors of 150 h.p., one motor fitted to each bogie. In addition to the regenerative braking the trailing axles are equipped with Westinghouse electro-pneumatic brakes.

When William Sebastian Graff-Baker suddenly collapsed and died outside his Kensington home in February 1952 at the age of 62, it brought to a sudden end an unprecedented era of amazingly original and inventive product development that was not to resurface for a further 30 years. In terms of the Underground, Frank Pick was indeed lucky to have had such a lieutenant in the organisation because no one other man had so much influence on the design and development of not only London Transport's rolling stock but also its lifts and escalators during its internationally acknowledged heyday.

He was born on 14 November 1889 and entered the service of the Metropolitan District Railway as a junior electrical fitter at the age of 20. He was appointed an assistant to the Mechanical Engineer in 1912 and a year later was placed in charge of all lifts and escalators on the London Electric Railway and the Central London Railway. After serving for a few months as the personal assistant to the Mechanical Engineer, he became Car Superintendent in 1921. A year later, he was appointed an officer of the Underground Group of Companies with the title of Assistant Mechanical Engineer. He continued to hold this after the formation of the London Passenger Transport Board in 1933, becoming Chief Mechanical Engineer (Railways) in 1934.

His obituary notice published on 18 February stated that: "he had a flair for invention and design and an astonishing fertility in the exercise of these qualities which amounted to genius. He was responsible for all of the major improvements in design which took place in London Transport's rolling stock, lifts and escalators such as more efficient automatic door equipment, faster and roomier trains and the improved car equipment design incorporated in the latest type of rolling stock. These all bear testimony to the ever fresh quality of mind and the greatness of his conception in design and invention. The new tube stock introduced on London Transport in 1938, with roller axle and suspension bearings and improved cam operated electrical equipment, represented one of his most important contributions to the design of electric rolling stock subjected to very arduous operating conditions".

He was by all accounts a man of wide general culture and interests with a deep appreciation of the visual arts.

He was also a likable, lively, challenging colleague, and a leader of men who was full of humanity and understanding. As a companion he was a jovial and lively conversationalist, and quick of repartee. The energy which he brought to everything he undertook was summed up by a colleague who said that no one in the Chief Mechanical Engineer's Department worked harder than the man at the head of it.

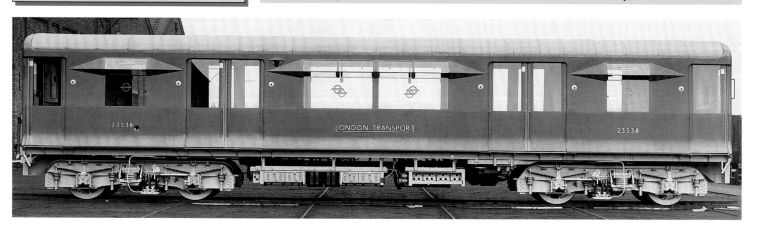

The development programme was put back again to be re-assessed in 1955 but London Transport's hand was forced by the Standard Stock, which needed urgent replacement because the oldest cars were now over 30 years old. It was agreed that three 7-car prototype trains, known as 1956 Stock, should be built and the first went into service on the Piccadilly Line in 1957. Positive experience with unpainted aluminium rather than steel bodies had already been gained on the post-war surface line R Stock cars and so these new tube stock trains were also left unpainted. The familiar LONDON TRANSPORT fleetname in Johnston typeface was retained, but the traditional gold transfers were replaced by red ones, edged with black to give greater contrast against the satin finished aluminium panelling.

Their successful trials prepared the way for large orders of 1959/1962 Stock which were used on the Piccadilly and Central Lines and remained in service between 30 to 40 years, certainly giving value for money to their owners. The 1962 Stock has only relatively recently been scrapped to make way for the new Central Line trains. Before the Northern Line trains were replaced by brand new vehicles leased from Metro-Cammell from mid-1998 onwards, travellers on the line were still riding on trains whose basic design was over 60 years old.

Below An artist's impression of the new tube stock showing the application of the then fashionable *speed whiskers* in red. Obviously the culture shock of trains left in their natural aluminium finish was considered by some to be too abrupt a change from the traditional red. This scheme never made it through to tube trains, but for several years it was a feature on unpainted surface stock, and red as a secondary colour continued to be discussed.

Below left and bottom left Similar *speed whiskers* had been felt to form a relief from solid coloured liveries and a way to teminate horizontal linings at train endings, seen here applied to a Southern Railway electric locomotive in 1942 and a British Railways diesel railcar in the 1950s. Their official purpose was to make their approach more visible to men working on the line.

Facing page top The roof treatment of driving motor car 40001 differed from the rest in that its beaded edge capped the cab front. The roofs of the three prototypes were initially left in natural aluminium finish, the traditional bitumastic grey paint being added some time later.

Facing page bottom Photographed when it had 20 years of service behind it, a Gloucester built unit leads a train at Finchley Central. The two units were instantly recognisable by the beading at the base of the windows.

These trains were in reality a 1938 Tube Stock Mk3, but with aluminium panels, fluorescent lights and the change from metal to rubber suspension which had required a considerable amount of development work. In terms of aesthetic design however, they confirmed the fact that real innovation was dormant. The engineers had, in the end, simply just rolled out the old 1938 Stock drawings again! Virtually every exterior and interior detail remained the same with none of the experimental innovatory ideas making it into production vehicles. The changes made which affected the passenger environment created an interior ambience that was inferior to 1938 Stock and not a step forward. It is interesting to reflect how such a situation would never be tolerated today as a result of the continuing rapid technological strides in every area, and the need to meet the ever increasing demands and expectations of passengers.

What were these changes? First of all the individual shaded tungsten lights with their art deco glass shades were replaced by close coupled fluorescent tubes in the centre of the ceiling. Because these were applied onto an existing design from a previous period, they had the appearance of an afterthought, rather than being fully integrated into the complete interior design as had been the case with the 1938 Stock.

The first of three 7-car aluminium bodied prototype 1956 Tube Stock trains which entered service on the Piccadilly Line in 1957 was built by Metro-Cammell. The vertical face of the cab top incorporating the destination display box and air inlet grilles was inherited from the 1952 mock-up. Otherwise these trains were visually very similar to the 1938 Stock. The roof treatment of the driving motor car followed the contours of the cab windows in a more satisfactory manner than on the other two prototypes – just like the 1938 Stock in fact!

Right Poster *Silver Trains* by Frank Overton 1960.

Below right Advertisement placed by Metropolitan-Cammell Carriage & Wagon Co. Ltd on front cover of 21st November 1958 issue of *Railway Gazette* featuring the interior of a 1956 Stock car.

Below left Souvenir tickets were promoted to ride on the new tube trains. The quoted 'additional space in a whole silver train . . . equal to an extra car of the present type is a comparison with Standard Stock, which shared the work on the Piccadilly with the 1938 Stock. The seating capacity of 1938 Stock and 1956 Stock was identical.

Below right One of the prototype trains in service at Piccadilly Circus.

The Piccadilly and Central Lines are being re-equipped with 1,200 new cars. This is part of a £30 million plan to replace Underground rolling stock. The new trains are lighter in weight, with an unpainted aluminium finish to save maintenance costs.

Other features are:
Rubber suspension.
Fluorescent lighting throughout.
More room in every train.

There will be more comfort for travellers on the Underground

THE SILVER TRAIN

Come and try the first of the new trains for the Piccadilly Line of London's Underground.

NO SPRINGS? Instead, 24 rubber pads that make you forget you're moving at all. The first train in Britain to do away with conventional steel springs.

WHEN THE LIGHTS GO ON, there are no dark spots. Sixty feet of fluorescent tube see to that.

SILVER TRAIN, because the aluminium alloy panelling is left unpainted. Each car is one ton lighter, so we save both paint and electric power.

PLENTY OF ROOM. The additional space in a whole silver train is equal to an extra car of the present type.

Special round trips are to be run from Acton Town to Hounslow West and back (non-stop) on every weekday (except Saturday) from Wednesday January 1st to Friday January 10th.

　　　＊　　　＊　　　＊

The Silver Train will leave Acton Town at 11.06, 11.46, 12.26, 1.26, 2.06, 2.46 and 3.26.

Fare 1/- (children under 14, 6d.)

Buy your Souvenir Tickets in advance at the Schoolboy's Own Exhibition (in the London Transport section of the British Transport Commission Stand), from the Travel Enquiry Offices at Piccadilly Circus and St. James's Park Underground Stations, or by post from the Fares and Charges Officer, London Transport, 55 Broadway, S.W.1. If you are writing please remember to say which day you wish to travel. You can buy tickets at any time from Acton Town Station.

The rich, welcoming colours of red and green, accented by varnished wood and chrome plate were replaced by blander tones of grey (plastic laminate and paint) although the same wooden surface finishes were retained. Over the years this colour scheme did not age as well as the traditional green surfaces and the interiors appeared increasingly drab and uninviting. Although the exposed tubes were very bright and a more cost effective solution in terms of power consumed, with their bland, cold light, they could never be as inviting as the original lighting scheme of 1938 Stock.

10 JANUARY 1958   SERIAL NO. 1149

THE SILVER TRAIN

special round trip between

ACTON TOWN and HOUNSLOW WEST

ADULT FARE 1/-

Issued subject to the bye-laws, regulations and conditions
of the London Transport Executive.

Below Photograph taken on 12th August 1957 showing Sir John Elliott, then Chairman of the London Transport Executive, shaking hands with Driver Sharpley bowing through the cab door, when the first of the prototype trains was shown to the press at Northfields station. The press release read – 'The trains will be of striking appearance having an all-silver exterior, representing a break-away from the traditional Underground red. Each set of seven units which comprise a train will cost £100,000 but will save many pounds, for the silver trains do not require painting'.

Facing page Interior of 1956 Stock on the Piccadilly Line. Apart from the close-coupled fluorescent lamps in the ceiling and the two sets of facing transverse seats, the only physical differences to 1938 Stock are the cast aluminium grab handles replacing the tubular bars above the transverse seats. On the production 1959 and 1962 stock cars, the depth of the seat cushions was reduced.

Above Another view of the stock when new. Although this purports to be taken in service, the car is obviously occupied by carefully posed LT employees of the time.

Left A colour view of the same style of interior in 1962 Stock taken in the 1980s.

Although most of the 1962 versions of these trains spent their entire life on the Central Line, there was another train type known as the 1960 Stock which was designed for this line, but whose further development was overtaken by events. This stock was intended to replace all the previously mentioned Standard Stock cars in use on the line and 12 prototype driving motor cars were built by Cravens of Sheffield, the first of these entering service at the end of 1960. Three 8-car trains were made up by using 12 reconditioned Standard Stock trailer cars which were all repainted silver to match the external panels of the 1960 Stock which, like the 1959 vehicles, were also of unpainted aluminium.

In design terms, these motor cars were very significant because they introduced several innovative features which had been totally lacking on the 1959/62 Stocks; some of which were to continue being incorporated in the final designs of coachbuilt tube stock in the 1980s. Most notable of these were the double width windows with interior casements of the same size which for the first time achieved a form of passenger saloon double glazing, albeit not sealed. Cravens presented this design approach in mock-up form to London Transport's engineers in the autumn of 1958. The retracting doors would now slide between the void that was created by this double walled construction, rather than into a localised door pocket structure fashioned for this purpose. This latter detail had been around since the earliest days of air operated doors and had also been followed through into the 1959/62 Stocks.

Above each window was a full length pull-down ventilator panel, the aluminium framing of which neatly incorporated the line diagram. As the illustration shows, this was a particularly neat piece of design integration since the corner radii and frame width of the extruded sections and trims were all related. Although the aim had been to reduce the amount of interior painting (melamine-faced panelling again being used) the ceiling was painted pegboard! This was done to improve levels of sound absorption but it is also an interesting detail which is very much of its period, borrowing as it does from contemporary architectural practice. There were several other well resolved features such as the position and continuity of the fluorescent lighting runs from car end to car end, the profile of the draught screens, the simple fixing details of the grab-poles, the generously ribbed aluminium, radiused bases of the transverse seats and the well integrated and pleasingly profiled handles at the

A relatively crude perspective sketch prepared in 1959 to show the proposed styling of the new 1960 Stock trains for the Central Line. It nonetheless shows quite dramatically the visual impact of the large double windows when seen at night and the slightly raked cab styling that was being envisioned.

One of the first 12 prototype driving motor cars hauling its rehabilitated Standard Stock trailers. The elusive character of the sketch was well captured in the final product, though the lines were less smooth. The external design of the double width windows would henceforth be perpetuated for the next 23 years on coachbuilt tube stock. The slightly raked back stance of the cab windows was effectively resolved by carrying through the body side crease line through to the front. The reconditioned Standard Stock trailer cars which were used to make up complete trains can be seen.

ends of the transverse seats (which were a good detail taken from the 1959/62 Stocks). Finally there was a very uncharacteristic LT moquette design, more akin to a settee of the period, and this effect was reinforced by covering the armrests in the same material! This was an interesting idea to promote a friendly, inviting interior. The design, flecked but otherwise plain, came in at least two colours – pink and yellow. The car interiors also featured Warerite laminates finished in different colours: some in pink and blue-grey, and others in green and yellow.

In an attempt to create a fresh styling for the front, the cab face was slightly raked. This feature was created by visually linking the crease along the body side with the cab's horizontal centre line. This characteristic body side crease had been a feature on all tube train types from Standard Stock onwards, which simply and neatly tailored the body side profile to fit the running tunnels. It would make its final appearance on the next generation of tube trains to be built (Victoria Line 1967 Stock), described in the next chapter. The front of the cab roof was again domed with echoes of the 1938 Stock and the air intake grille was neatly positioned behind the destination box.

Although these trains were intended to be the forerunners of a completely new fleet for the Central Line, the overall condition of the line's Standard Stock trains of late 1920s and early 1930s vintage did not allow the luxury of an intensive service testing period. Another problem was the greater than expected cost of converting the Standard Stock trailers. For these reasons a repeat order was made of the tried and tested 1959 Stock design for the line.

Two views of the interior mock-up for the 1960 Stock that was built by Cravens and presented to London Transport in the autumn of 1958. Two alternative surrounds for the route map were offered, the radiused version being chosen for production vehicles.

The interior of 1960 Stock when new. There is an overall softness and harmony in the detailing which remains very acceptable today: this important customer friendly character was to be missing in subsequent designs up to the early 1980s. The 'smoothly' profiled moquette covered armrests and the generously radiused seat bases add to this effect and the fluorescent lamp housings that illuminate the pegboard ceiling are pleasingly detailed and well integrated within the total design. The neat innovative double glazed window treatment which created the housing for the retracting sliding door is also well illustrated.

Right Close-up of the peg board ceiling and the neat fluorescent lighting runs.

Below The pink and blue-grey interior, photographed in the autumn of 1964.

Bottom right An object lesson in integrated design. The unique treatment of the line diagram framing which completed the overall radiused form of the windows when viewed from inside.

Bottom left Another nice touch. Ventilation was achieved by pulling forward the line diagram panel.

The interior of one of the Standard Stock trailer cars which were 'modernised' to run with 1960 Stock with fluorescent lighting and polished stainless steel handrails.

Because of the urgency of replacing the Central Line's Standard Stock, the 7-car 1959 Tube Stock trains that were being delivered to the Piccadilly Line were instead diverted (from train 20 onwards) to the Central Line and an order was placed with Metro-Cammell to make these trains up to 8-cars.

In addition, an order was placed for more trains (like 1959 Tube Stock) with the Birmingham Railway Carriage & Wagon Company, but they went into liquidation (believed to be due to quoting too low for this contract) and that order was then transferred to Metro-Cammell who were also building 1959 Tube Stock. Once the 1962 Tube Stock (as this new batch was called) came on stream, the 7-car 1959 Tube Stock trains were transferred to the Piccadilly Line.

These 1960 Stock vehicles had a chequered history. Five were converted to full Automatic Train Operation (ATO) at the end of 1963 and sufficient pioneering experience was then gained operationally by running in this mode on the Central Line Hainault to Woodford section to enable the system to become a key feature of the forthcoming 1967 Stock Victoria Line trains then being specified. Two driving motor cars of 1960 Stock still live on today forming part of a 3-car Track Recording Train and another two are preserved.

Photograph taken in 1961 with passengers on board, complete with Liz Frazer look-alike about to leave the train.

CHAPTER FIVE

The years 1967 to 1983

TUBE TRAINS

Pre-eminent among British design consultancies during the 1950s and the 1960s was Design Research Unit and their growth and influence during this period was due to the drive and charismatic personality of one of their founding partners, Professor Sir Misha Black. He was a Consultant to the Board of London Transport from 1964 to 1977 and was originally invited to become a member of their Design Panel in 1963, originally set up to advise on design issues concerning the new Victoria Line, the first brand new tube railway line in London for 60 years. Apart from Professor Black, the original membership consisted of the Board's Architect, K. Seymour, the Chief Publicity Officer, Harold Hutchison, and was under the chairmanship of Mr Eric Ottaway, whose guiding hand had shaped and influenced some of London Transport's finest pre- and post-war bus and coach designs.

Misha Black was later invited to extend his consultancy to include all aspects of London Transport design but, as we shall see, the terms of reference for the Panel in this wider role were very loosely constructed and, as a result, their influence and impact was piecemeal notwithstanding some major design successes that were achieved. In rolling stock terms there remain to this day DRU's strong influence on the external visual design of the 1967, 1972, 1973 Tube and the D78 Surface Stock types, all of them built by Metro-Cammell.

Probably their greatest contribution to the development of tube trains was the work that they did with the engineers at Acton Works in evolving the then novel cab design with its generously radiused corners and wrap-round cab windows for the 1967 Victoria Line stock. Misha Black and James (Jim) Williams (in 1967 to become Partner at DRU with responsibility for a newly created product design group) developed a good working relationship with Stan Driver, at the time Chief Draughtsman. Stan headed the rolling stock design office at Acton Works and was very receptive and supportive of fresh concepts. This cab styling treatment would give these trains a dynamic progressive style that was completely appropriate to the fact that they were the first metro trains in the world to incorporate full automatic train operation technology (ATO). By the middle of 1964 a partial length full size mock-up for the new train design had been prepared and notes of Informal Design Panel Meeting No.13 written in September of that year state that "an original attempt to run the front profile round into the side profile gave a skewed look to the front window, and a modification had been agreed which would set this window in its own plane." In the minutes of Informal Meeting No. 14 issued at the end of that month, 'Joe' Manser reported that: "the front end cab design had been altered to overcome the impression of distortion by changing the radius of curvature of the window and the window line of the body side as a result of visits to Metro-Cammell by Professor Black and himself."

The large saloon windows with their crisp crease line below were inherited from innovative design of 1960 stock but Jim Williams and Stan Driver persuaded the manufacturers to punch these windows into a sheer and smoothly profiled body side. This smooth appearance was enhanced by treating the required ventilation inlets as simple rectangular slots which were aligned above them. This was a definitive step forward in design terms because the tops of the windows on 1960 Stock were obscured by deeply cowled ventilation louvres. The image that these trains gave when new was akin to a satin anodised aluminium cigar tube with all of their required features and elements pierced into it. The fact that there were no cab doors (the train operator entering through a door in the passenger saloon) also contributed to their very smooth

An early idea being considered at Acton for Victoria Line cabs was a return to the central driving position of the streamlined 1935 Stock. The mock-up of this arrangement is shown below and dates from about 1962. The exact reasons for this idea are unknown, but as it was the intention early on to have the trains automatically operated, the on-board staff member would have better visibility from a central position. Improved visibility was, in the event, provided by wrap-round windscreens on the final design.

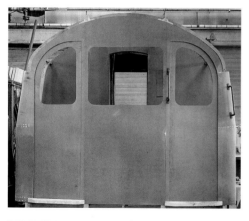

Above This early design approach for Victoria Line stock is a blend of features taken from 1960 Stock and the front end of 1959/62 Stock. Taller door windows are, however, already present.

Left Following the mock-up with a central driving position, a second one was built around the middle of 1963 based on the above sketch. This reverted to a conventional centre cab access door and the cab windows at this stage were still intended to be made from flat glass. The photograph shows that experiments to configure a satisfactory final shape for them are still in hand and the shape of the roof dome is still unresolved.

Below In 1964 the ideas of some students from the Royal College of Art were exhibited in the booking hall of Charing Cross station. A full size mock-up of a section of the interior was shown alongside a model of the exterior. By this time, wrap-round windscreens had been proposed by DRU and the students would no doubt have been informed of this. One of their suggestions for the interior was for illuminated line diagrams above the car cards (seen here as plain lighting panels).

Above Final ideas take shape in this mid-1964 mock-up, though a number of subtle changes were to be made before the trains went into production.

Above right Close-up of the wrap-round cab windows on the same mock-up. No side cab doors were fitted, so that the driver would be prevented from getting out of the cab with operating equipment set to automatic.

Right Front end view of a production cab.

The exterior of the mock-up showing the tangent radiused ends to the ventilation slots which harmonised nicely with the corner radii of the windows. It was decided to square these off for the production vehicles, but this pleasing visual feature would return once again to be used on the Piccadilly Line's 1973 Stock.

exterior form. There was some very nice detailing in this area where the side window was let into an aluminium casting which was skilfully blended with its surrounding sheet aluminium metalwork. Another inspired piece of integrated design was the incorporation of the train whistles into one of the external cab door grab handles!

A yellow 'calling on' light which could be illuminated to call on a following train to give assistance, was fitted at the top right hand side of the cab. The totem UNDERGROUND in red Johnston capitals replaced the previous LONDON TRANSPORT logotype on the body sides.

Regarding the interior design of the vehicles, DRU were unfortunately not able to influence the detail design of all the fixtures and fittings as they would have wished because their remit was to do concept and general arrangement drawings only. These were then handed over to the mechanical engineers and designers at Acton who would then agree the development and implementation details with the manufacturer. DRU however, certainly influenced the integration of the fluorescent lighting tubes within the ceiling profile by recommending that these should be mounted within rectangular recesses. This lighting was augmented for the first time by illuminated advertisement frames. These were not satisfactorily integrated with the non illuminated ones and thus always appeared to be the design afterthought that they were! They also were a different size to the non-illuminated ones (which always looked odd) which meant that two sizes of advertisements were required. Advertisers tended not to supply these, hence small adverts were put into larger frames which made matters worse. They also proved to be a maintenance liability over the years because the all-pervading tunnel dust built up in the corners and more often than not they just remained unilluminated.

Interior views of the cab mock-up and the finalised production version clearly demonstrate the enhanced wide-angle view which the driver enjoyed through these cab windows. This certainly was a great step forward in terms of outward visibility as shown by the comparative shot of a 1960 Stock cab.

A design success, however, was DRU's development of a two-tier armrest design which was hailed at the time of launch of these trains as enabling adjacent passengers each to have their own individual space. These were an attractive evolution from strangely ugly prototypes of the concept, suggested by a passenger, that had been trialled during the 1960s in 1938 Stock cars.

The draughtscreen designs were only a small evolutionary step from those seen in the 1960 Stock. Indeed, the detailing of all of the interior castings, although extremely workmanlike, lacked any visual flair; DRU were not consulted on the development of these, neither did they have any involvement in the cab interior. They were usually just presented with a *fait accompli* in these areas when LT staff visited the manufacturer's premises, and DRU would be informed that there was no longer any time to change anything! Unlike in later years, there was no interest shown by LT in experimenting with areas such as alternative positions and designs for handrails and grabpoles. Indeed the notes of Design Panel Meeting No.15 held on 21st December 1964 stated that, following an inspection of the mock-up by LT's Vice-Chairman, Anthony Bull: "it was considered that the present shape and layout of grab handles, with which satisfactory experience has been obtained for many years, should be retained".

Misha Black had wanted, in September 1964, to commission a new moquette pattern from a professional designer arguing that "since there would be many features of the new line which appear to be the same as others in the passengers' eyes and because the seats in trains were so prominent to the eye, it would be one place to demonstrate the newness of the line." He lost his argument at the end of the year because Eric Ottaway stated that: "Whilst a new design of moquette for the Victoria

Above The superbly clean *cigar tube* type styling of the production trains when new, with the square ended ventilation slots above each window. The lack of a side entrance door for the train operator contributed to the sleek, uncluttered design. The fully glazed doors inherited from the 'sunshine' car of the late 1940s, and championed by Alec Valentine (by now knighted and chairman of London Transport) finally made their appearance on a production train.

Bottom left and centre Two close up views of the masterly blending of aluminium castings and sheet metalwork.

Bottom right The cab door handles incorporating the train whistle.

Line cars would make a favourable impression on passengers, it was not possible at this time, in view of the large number of railway moquettes already in use, to add yet another". What a difference in attitude to that which currently prevails where every line has its own dedicated pattern! It was nonetheless agreed at the same meeting that a new design which could be used for either road or rail purposes could be evolved and three designers were put forward by Misha Black (Marianne Straub, Jacqueline Groag and The Orbit Design Group) to submit designs for a fee of 50 guineas (£52.50) each for the production of preliminary designs with a final fee of 200 guineas (£210.00) for the one chosen to go into production.

The outcome of this was that a new blue/green design by Marianne Straub was approved in May 1965 but it was then already too late to specify its use on the Victoria Line trains. The red, black and grey one developed for A Stock was used instead. Her pattern was eventually used in great quantity on various tube and surface stock trains from the late 1960s and the early 1970s.

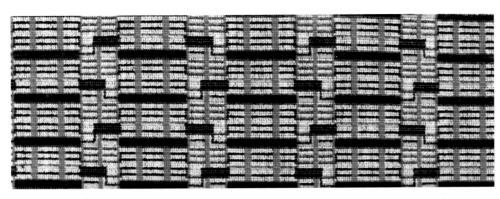

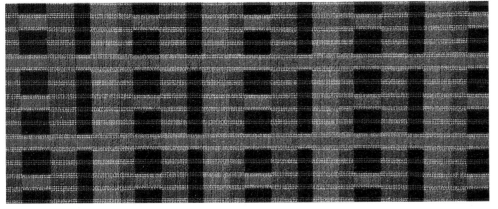

Top and above Despite the modern exterior, seen being inspected by Misha Black and colleagues on the project, the story inside was very much the same as before. The view of the interior of a brand new train was taken in 1968 and reveals a disappointing lack of any real innovation, apart from DRU's recessed light tube and their two-tiered armrest design. The moquette pattern was inherited by default from the A60/62 Stock trains.

Above left The red, black and grey moquette of existing design that was used in 1967 Stock.

Left The blue/green moquette pattern designed by Marianne Straub which arrived too late to be used in the Victoria Line trains.

The all-pervading grey and aluminium interiors of these trains, which so closely recalled the look of the platforms and lower concourse areas of the stations, was exactly in keeping with the industrial design spirit of the times. This was in direct contrast to the exuberant use of colour and highly fashionable and ephemeral shapes that were generally being advocated elsewhere during this period. It is to DRU's credit that they refused to be influenced by these transitory influences and maintained an ordered, calm approach that remained true to Frank Pick's principles of being fit for purpose. This was unlike the Berlin Underground whose consultant architects wholeheartedly espoused highly fashionable solutions for their new lines built during the same period and which now appear extremely hackneyed and dated. It could also be said with some justification that the Victoria Line stations with their tones of grey on grey now look just dull and boring! It was Misha Black's view that these stations need only serve as a backdrop to the passengers themselves who would then supply the required colour and movement.

The 1949 London Plan Working Party Report which had proposed the Victoria Line also recommended the construction of another new cross-town tube railway connecting up with the Baker Street to Stanmore section of the Bakerloo Line. This became known as the Fleet Line and financial approval was granted in 1971 for the first stage between Baker Street and Charing Cross which would give much needed relief to the in-town section of the Bakerloo Line. Construction began the following year and the original plans showed further stages of the new line extending to New Cross Gate and Lewisham via Ludgate Circus in the City. The scheme was however cut back for financial reasons and Charing Cross remained the new line's terminus. The works were well advanced by 1977 and although it actually did get within 400 yards or so of Fleet Street, it was decided to change the name to the Jubilee Line to mark the Queen's Silver Jubilee in that year.

Facing page A general interior view and detail shot, the latter taken when new in early 1968. Central Line diagrams are in position on this photograph because the Hainault loop was equipped for automatic working and most of the trains were tested there. Also it can be seen that, at the car ends, there was no standback at all against the bulkhead (unlike on earlier trains). This could be an inconvenience for standing passengers who could not tuck themselves out of the way during busy traffic periods. This user feature would reappear with the advent of 1973 Stock. The illuminated advertisement panels differed in size and presentation to the un-illuminated ones, thus creating an unco-ordinated appearance. DRU had no influence on the shape and positioning of both panels within the interior design; they were pushed through by others. Indeed, Misha Black stated, in a Design Panel review meeting in September 1964, that they would not enhance the design of the car and that they should not be adopted unless the financial benefits were considerable.

Above The line diagram panels hinged down in order to augment saloon ventilation. The idea was borrowed from the innovative interior of the 1960 Stock, but in time would become a pronounced customer unfriendly feature, for standing passengers could look straight into a void made dirty by the accumulation of the all-pervading tunnel dust.

Below left The design quality of the armrests stands out against the prosaic detailing of everything else.

Below right Their inspiration! The trial of these modified two-tier armrests was carried out during the early 1960s on 1938 Stock.

Facing page The two renderings produced by Peter Ashmore, the celebrated British industrial designer, for Design Research Unit. These proposed replacing the wrap-round cab windows with a more simple treatment which involved only slight curvature of the cab windows. DRU's proposal to repaint the doors red once again would be reserved for the 1972 Mk 2 Tube trains only, but they would return 20 years later, together with the full red front as part of the finally chosen corporate livery for painted trains. The second rendering suggested how extended cab access rails could be painted red as a design feature.

Below A scale model prepared by Jim Williams of Design Research Unit in the autumn of 1968 for what would have been a further generation of new trains for what was then known as the Fleet Line.

Bottom The way designs were developed in those days. Jim Williams hard at work at DRU's Ayebrook Street offices using the time honoured drafting tools of set-square, tee-square and lots of drafting tape.

Originally, another new fleet of trains was planned to service the new line in its entirety and Design Research Unit were again asked by the LT Board to provide design advice for both the rolling stock and the new tunnel platforms. Reproduced is a photograph of a model designed by Jim Williams showing how further cab treatments were being explored. Developing the wrap-round cab window concept and separating the roof from the cab front by stepping it back were initial ideas that were investigated but were dropped at an early stage. The indicated powered sliding side access door for the train operator would however make an appearance sometime later.

The two airbrushed perspectives (right) show two later proposals for how these trains might have looked. They were prepared by Peter Ashmore, who with his partner Edward 'Ted' Wilkes, had been one of Britain's pioneer industrial design consultancies on transportation design projects since the end of the Second World War. Wilkes & Ashmore were, together with DRU, the design consultants on the majority of locomotives and passenger train interiors that had been designed for British Rail throughout the 1960s. These included the London Midland main line electric locomotives, the Hymek and Deltic locos, the Western Region Warship and Western class locos and the Type 4 diesel-electrics that eventually became the Class 47s – still to be seen in everyday service at the start of the 21st century.

It is interesting that at this stage (probably as a result of pressure from the engineers at Acton Works!) they were now proposing to move away from the wrap-round cab windows of the 1967 Tube Stock to a simpler solution contained within the contour of a softly profiled cab front. The high cost of the Victoria Line stock's cab windows has always been an issue and DRU had clearly been asked to examine cheaper alternatives. In the event, wrap-round cab windows would be retained for one final brand new design of tube stock. Significantly the red cab treatment on the front of the train together with the red doors pre-date what would be chosen as the greater part of the Underground's corporate livery some 20 years later. The alternative view shows just the cab door access handrails picked out in red.

In the end, because of the reduction of the new line's original length, virtually the same 1967 Tube Stock design was rolled out for the 1972 Mark 1 and Mark 2 trains. Both types were used on the Northern Line and the latter vehicles also provided the rolling stock requirements for stage one of the Jubilee Line when it finally opened to the public in May 1979. There was, at this time, much political manoeuvring taking place which was behind the development of both batches of 1972 Tube Stock and also the 1973 Tube Stock; this had the effect of shunting the 1959 Tube Stock from the Piccadilly onto the Northern Line where it was to stay until the start of its replacement in late 1998.

The only reason why 1972 Mk 1 Stock was built was because Horace Cutler (then Leader of the Greater London Council which had been handed control of London Transport in 1970) offered money to put trains "like those on the Victoria Line" onto the Northern to relieve its long-standing Misery Line tag. He wanted an existing design quickly and was willing to pay – so there was no contest.

1972 Mk 2 was again a political stock in that the government persuaded LT to fill a gap in Metro-Cammell's order book by ordering some trains that would eventually run on the Jubilee Line. Scrapping of 1938 Tube Stock, new stock on the Piccadilly for Heathrow, the Jubilee Line and the politics above all else led to a chaotic era for new stock and stock allocation. As a result, aesthetic design fell to a low level of priority.

A 1972 Mark 2 train with bus red doors and red silhouette roundel; two recommendations from DRU's *London Transport's Design Survey* document of June 1971 that were actioned.

The absence of cab doors on these trains would become profoundly inconvenient in service use because (unlike the Victoria Line) crew changes occurred at stations where trains were packed and the unfortunate driver just could not get out. When they eventually appeared on the Jubilee Line some 'bodges' were made so that he could escape through the front door and onto the platform using grab rails and step plates; this was however impossible on the Northern Line because the platforms were too short. This is an example of some of the unfortunate knock-on effects that can occur when trains are designed in panic mode!

Because of the platform lengths on the Northern and Bakerloo lines, all 1972 Tube Stock was built as 7- rather than 8-car trains. Two-person operation was normal at the time so both Mark 1 and Mark 2 batches had the traditional guard's operating control panels at the trailing end of the passenger compartment of driving motor cars. In addition, as it was expected that the Mark 2 trains would eventually run on a one-person operated (OPO) automatic Jubilee Line, these were also provided when new with door controls in the cab as well. In the event, Mk 2 trains were converted to OPO for use on the Bakerloo Line but never went automatic. The Mark 1 vehicles mirrored the 1967 Stock in every way, with the identical moquette being used, but the Mark 2s received the red doors and a red silhouette roundel from DRU's initial proposals; however the attractive red front was abandoned. The new blue/green moquette pattern was used and this was to become a very familiar pattern on various stocks and also on buses. The armrests were also changed from red to blue to visually relate with the new fabric.

The use of a simple red silhouette LT roundel (i.e. without the supporting message Underground) on the sides of trains arose out of a proposal made by DRU in a London Transport Design Survey document issued in June 1971. They recommended that since this silhouette roundel clearly represented "Transport in London" it should henceforth be used to brand all of LT's passenger vehicles; in red on natural aluminium trains and in white on red buses and trains, in the same size.

In order to reinforce one single tone of red as the basic LT house colour, they also proposed that the lighter and brighter 'bus red' should be used on all painted road and rail vehicles, arguing that the traditional darker tone of 'train red' should henceforth be jettisoned. They saw this colour as an unnecessarily depressing alternative to the bus red. This policy was then only actioned in a piecemeal fashion over the following years with the following results.

No doubt for reasons of cost, it was not systematically applied to the train fleet; with the result that, as far as the passengers were concerned, a confusing mixed bag of graphic brands LONDON TRANSPORT, UNDERGROUND and the red roundel) would be seen on the sides of trains for a further 20 years until a painted corporate

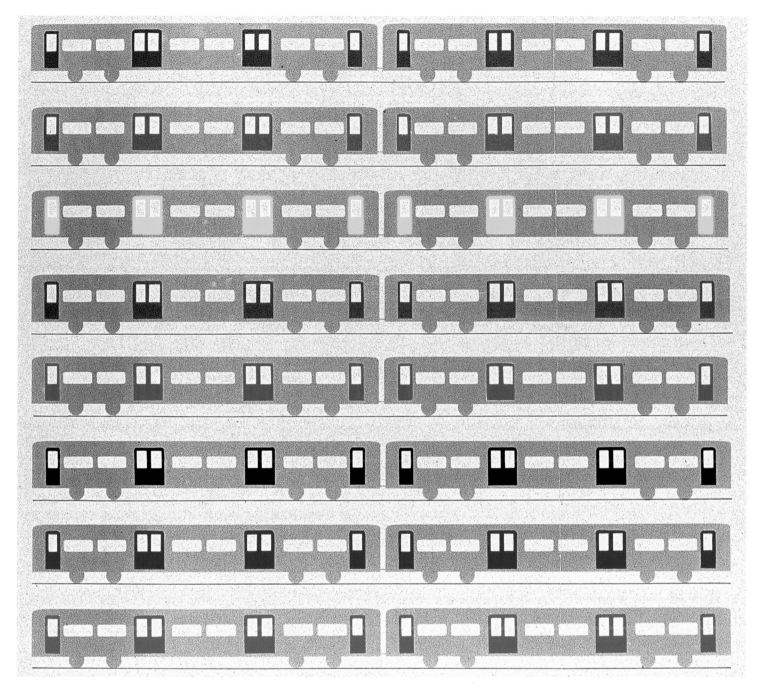

Underground livery was finally applied (see later chapters). Furthermore bus red never looked quite right when it was applied to the painted 1938 Tube and CO/CP Stock trains still in service during the 1970s. Trains that were repainted in this colour also featured white silhouette roundels and car numbers which replaced the classic traditional gold transfers. Unfortunately this step significantly devalued the quality of the appearance, for the final result looked somewhat mean and penny-pinching in its presentation and was certainly a sharp fall from former glories. It also justified the original decision to use the darker red – which was decided upon in Frank Pick's day.

The same report also illustrated some interesting design concepts for the exterior treatment of trains. One of these shows a solution to the perennial problem of passengers needing reassurance that they are boarding the correct train for their required line by colouring the doors in the respective line colour. An interesting idea but killed off at the time by the requirements to make stock available for different lines.

The issue of line related colour schemes for rolling stock then lay dormant for a full 20 years until it was again resurrected following the establishment of individual Line Managers who became fully responsible for every aspect of their line's business performance. We shall see how the subject was tackled again in a later chapter.

Illustration taken from DRU's 1971 *Design Survey* document showing a proposal to paint the doors of rolling stock in each line colour, which they argued 'would certainly increase the visual effectiveness of rolling stock'. They, of course, had to add the rider that 'it would need to be decided on the basis of cost effectiveness whether this would justify the additional initial and maintenance expenditure'. The trains are shown in the order: Bakerloo, Central, Circle, District, Metropolitan, Northern, Piccadilly and Victoria.

Above Partial length full size mock-up of 1973 Tube Stock at Acton Works before the amendments made to the shape of the cab side windows. As can be seen by the comparative view of a production train opposite, these subtle changes resulted in a significant improvement to the cab styling.

Below Very much 'more of the same' for the interior of the 1973 Stock, as shown by this mock-up photographed in the middle of 1971 at Acton Works.

Following authority for the construction of the extension of the Piccadilly Line into the heart of Heathrow airport, consideration had to be given to what stock to use. The existing 1959 Stock then operating on the Line was still relatively new but unsuitable for the extended service which would generate additional traffic. A greater number of trains would be required and they would have to cope with air travellers' luggage, the stowage of which was seen as a major problem. New trains were the answer and 1959 Stock would transfer to the Northern Line.

The design of these new trains began in 1970. Each car was to be six feet longer than cars of earlier types but the total length of each 6-car train would still be about 17 feet shorter than a typical seven car train of 1959 Stock. The door leaves were now top-hung. On all previous air door tube stocks, the door weight was carried in bottom tracks using two basic sytems – either flanged wheels running on a rail inside a gap within the door step casting or rollers, with improved guidance, acting on a bearing surface on the door step. Air operated cab doors, which could be operated independently from the passenger doors, were fitted for the first time on tube stock. Also a 'selective door close' mechanism was fitted which enabled the guard to close all except one single door and one single leaf of a double door if the weather was poor at terminal stations. The stock was originally two-person operated but was converted to one-person operation during 1987, after which the driver performed this function.

The first train entered service in July 1975 as a passenger carrying special when the extension to Hatton Cross was opened and the first normal passenger service started one month later.

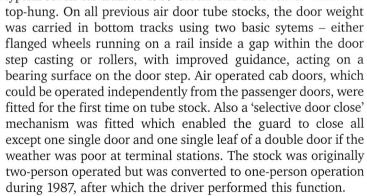

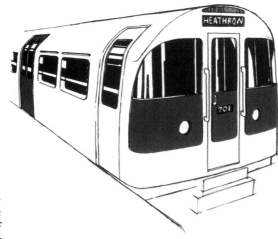

Design Research Unit were again the industrial design advisors for this stock and the photograph opposite shows the cab-end mock up at Acton Works. In terms of the external appearance of these trains, they represented the ultimate development of the visual quality of the classic 1938 Stock coachbuilt design. The proportions of the cab are particularly pleasing since they were a very subtle development from those established for the 1967 and 1972 stocks. Interestingly, minutes of a meeting held at Acton Works in January 1971 between Stan Driver, Misha Black and Jim Williams note that: "It was felt that the shape of the front side windows could be slightly improved by a better relationship between their top edges and the roof line. It was agreed that it was not necessary to alter the mock-up and that the modification could be made on the working drawings". Examination of the production cab design shows that this change was in fact made to the considerable benefit of the final appearance, and DRU also advised on the proportion and execution of the painted panel (in train red after all!) on the front of the cab. Another series of sketches show how line colours could be applied onto train fronts in an integrated manner that was incorporated into the structural form and not superficially applied as an afterthought.

An article written by a notable design journalist, Martin Pawley, in the 15th April 1987 edition of the *Architects' Journal*, celebrated the style of these trains and eulogised over the perfection of their detailing. He said:

"The advanced engineering of the 1973 Tube Stock, designed specifically for the Piccadilly Line Heathrow link and the first made to a life cycle costed specification, was a breakthrough in the design of underground railways. This combines with the timeless styling of its low profile, clean lines and simple aluminium finish to represent the highest and most exhilarating achievement of functional modern design in the Underground.

"The 1973 Tube Stock has another distinction apart from its advanced engineering. Notwithstanding design parameters as rigorous in their way as those

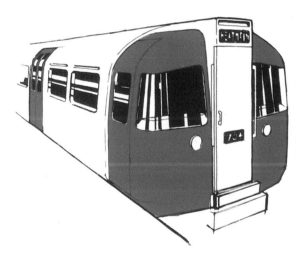

Left The red lower front panel of this 1973 Stock train was applied as a result of a suggestion by the Design Panel to 'increase the impact of the new Piccadilly Line stock by painting a red heralding patch on its nose'. DRU's view was that, although helpful, this had been added as an afterthought and therefore was at least partially an admission of failure in the basic design of the car. Nonetheless, it has to be said that the application of this coloured panel was surprisingly successful in visual terms, adding considerably to the train's character.

Above To clarify their point further, DRU produced these three illustrations in their *Design Report* of 1971, showing how the nose detail of 1973 could still have been amended so that the approved colour patch was incorporated within its structural form and not superficially applied.

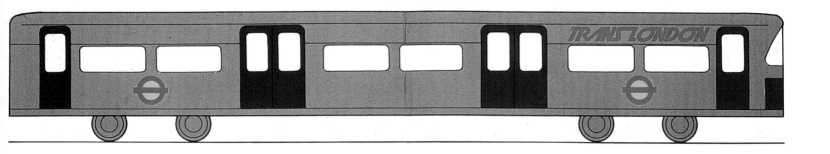

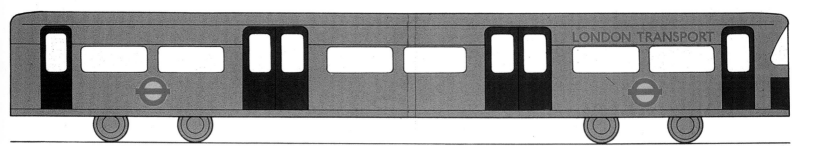

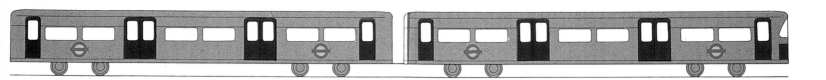

The *Design Report* of 1971 also proposed that the Piccadilly Line should be differentiated from others as being the direct link between central London and the World via Heathrow. They therefore suggested bold aircraft-type identification above the windows on the first car, arguing that (with the introduction of train washing machines) this was now possible as the roof, as well as the carbody sides, would be regularly washed. A special name might be devised for the line such as Trans London, presented in a distinctive logotype. At that time a red and yellow roundel was also being proposed by them as a pan-LT design solution for both bus and rail applications with the blue colour only to be retained for limited applications such as the doors of the Piccadilly Line trains. As a development of this proposal, yellow on red would also gradually replace the white on blue back-illuminated fascias to Underground stations.

applied to 12 metre yachts and jet airliners, and an operating environment no less punishing, the Piccadilly Line train is a tremendous and timeless styling success. The full beauty of the design can best be seen on the long surface runs out to Heathrow, where the trains touch 60 mph and their big automobile-style wrap round windscreens, long cars and low tunnel-fitting profile and natural aluminium finish still lend them the electric excitement of a secret prototype – a decade after the line was opened."

He continued: "Earlier tube stock featured clumsy hopper ventilation windows, projecting window-head rainwater drips, truncated ventilator slots, thick door retraction reveals, or some other stylistic imperfection".

"While 1973 Tube Stock arguably represents the highest achievement of functional design in the Underground, its perfection is not the unalloyed result of rational technology. Indeed if that were the sole criterion it would be difficult to fault the claim of 1960 Tube Stock . . . The true design merit of 1973 Tube Stock resides in the tiny acts of artifice that accompany its first class engineering, enabling that which is already simplified to appear to be even simpler than it is". Pawley was particularly impressed with the following details on the trains:

"In the case of the 1973 Tube Stock, the most subtle example of enhanced simplicity is the 'lost' reveal that accommodates the decreased width of the ends of the cars." Each car is tapered over the last metre of its length, where the end doors are situated, in order to accommodate the tight track curves of the line. In plan the taper is achieved by an elegant 'lost' rebate detail that also accommodates the termination of the hollow recesses which form the door retraction recesses. "Another, even more crucial to the appearance of the whole train, is the dummy ventilation extension above the car windows. On the two preceding tube stock designs, the Victoria Line's 1967 ATO trains, and the Northern Line's 1972 Mark 1 and 2 stocks, the ventilator slit

above the car windows stops short at the commencement of the door retraction reveal. On 1973 Stock, the black slit of the ventilator on the outside is carried across the retracted door position in the form of a black painted recess in the aluminium outer skin. The result is a visual logic that enhances the engineering and operating logic of the cars themselves. It may pass unnoticed by the million people a day who travel on the Piccadilly Line, but once you become aware of it you can never fail to appreciate the subtlety of the design of Underground trains again".

In truth the excellence of its exterior design was not matched by the quality of its interior design. It was certainly workmanlike enough but was totally derivative of previous solutions. DRU were very disappointed that comments from the Design Panel were invited only at a stage where only minor modifications could be accepted and quite frankly this showed.

Another view of this handsome stock when new.

Inset The Queen inspecting the interior of the train when the link to Heathrow Central was officially opened in December 1977. The blue and green moquette makes another appearance, but sadly the overall design quality of the interior does not match that of the exterior. It is obvious from the derivative nature of its design that DRU had been totally excluded from the development process. Because of the ongoing technical problems that were being experienced with the ventilation fans as originally specified, they still had not been fitted to this car some two years after the trains had first gone into service.

Left and below left Two of the design details so much admired by Martin Pawley. The dummy ventilation extension above the car windows and the 'lost' reveal accommodating the decreased width of the car ends.

Bottom left The deeper standback spaces that were provided next to the doorways to accommodate luggage. This was, at best, a very half-hearted solution to a pressing problem.

Bottom centre Close-up of one of the ugly ventilation fans and the generally unco-ordinated detailing of the interior.

Bottom right An example of 'customer unfriendly' detailing!

What was originally seen as a great problem to supply sufficient luggage space for travellers was in the end solved by simply specifying deeper than normal standback spaces at the car ends and in the double doorway positions. This was never really successful, particularly in a crowded train because people like to be able to keep in touch, or at least see their luggage at all times! We will see in a later chapter how this important convenience feature for the airport bound passengers was given considerable attention, 20 years on.

The same minutes of the January 1971 meeting at Acton Works with Stan Driver of LT and Misha Black and Jim Williams of DRU show that the overall grey colour scheme with pale yellow end walls was a DRU recommendation to the Design Panel. Interestingly this same yellow had also originally been proposed for the door surrounds and the internal door faces as well, but these ended up in grey. The same blue and green moquette used on the 1972 Mark 2s was again specified but the impact of the interior with its slightly angled stainless steel grabpoles was very much as before, except that some of the detailing was an unfortunate step backwards instead of forwards. The draughtscreens against the longitudinal seat bays were decreased in depth to create greater access to these areas but this meant that the traditional generous radiating of these screens, which had been a feature of tube trains since the days of 1938 Tube Stock, was replaced by a small cast detail with a particularly customer-unfriendly sharp edge. Three ventilation fans per car were part of the original specification but there were considerable difficulties in achieving a satisfactory design and these were fitted later in the production programme and were not operational until late 1977. Problems still persisted and they were finally decommissioned but they remained in their ugly housings until the trains were refurbished. The ventilation slots with their actuating controls also appeared harsh and crude.

Since it can confidently be said that the exterior (though not interior) design of the Piccadilly Line's 1973 Tube Stock represented the absolute pinnacle in the gradual development of the original ground-breaking 1938 Stock design concept, it was truly surprising that the next generation of tube train design, the 1983 Stock for the Jubilee Line, was such a backward step in terms of its visual appearance. However, to prove that every cloud has a silver lining the general reaction to these trains, and particularly that of the then LT Design Committee, would usher in the era of Industrial Design Consultants who, henceforce, were to be retained and fully involved with the design and development of any new trains for the Underground.

What had gone wrong? We have already seen the design background for the rolling stock that was to serve the original full length Fleet Line (later known as the Jubilee Line) at the start of the 1970s, which was originally expected to require 60 new trains. The decision not to build the line beyond Charing Cross reduced the number of trains required to 33. These would directly replace the 1972 Mark 2 Stock which could then be transferred to the Bakerloo Line (where they still operate today). The Underground system was also experiencing, at the end of the 1970s, a steady decline in ridership as a result of fare increases and so, as a result of all of this, only 15 new 6-car trains were ordered from Metro-Cammell in 1981 and existing stock spread slightly thinner over the rest of the system. The urgent need was to get rid of the worst of the 1938 Stock, and the minimum number of trains which would allow this was 15. The other half of the Jubilee Line fleet was made up of 1972 Mk 2s.

Below The totally unremarkable front end of the 1983 Stock shown in a mock-up at Acton Works in 1980. Shallower front glazing had earlier been planned, with the bottom edge aligning with the top of the driver's console.

Right Interior mock-up of 1983 Stock before fitting of armrests.

Below right The elegantly simple door area of the mock-up where grabpoles and the over door handrail were formed from one continuously cranked length of tubular section. Unfortunately, this treatment was soon replaced by the traditional method of separating out the horizontal and vertical elements . In this instance it seemed to have been overlooked that straight grabpoles play a very important role in maintaining structural integrity when anchored to a coachbuilt carbody structure in this location. Without them the cars wobbled and sagged to the point where they could become out of gauge when loaded.

For the first time ever on any tube train design before or since, the corners of the front of the 1983 Stock bore no visual relationship whatsoever with the shaping at the car ends. The cab face was absolutely flat with a sharp corner radius that was totally at odds with the car's generously shaped and radiused rear which echoed that of the 1972 Stock. The handsome wrap-round cab windows from the 1967/72/73 Stocks were now replaced by flat panels of newly-specified missile-proof glass, which is extremely expensive to produce in a curved form.

The double width windows and the radiusing around the door apertures were lifted straight from the original 1960 Stock design and the elegantly proportioned air intake slots from the 1973s were this time enlarged in an attempt to gain more in-car ventilation; their appearance becoming cruder as a result with no measurable improvement in performance. (It has been said that the only tube cars that have ever provided really efficient through-train ventilation in tunnel working were the gate stock vehicles from before the First World War!)

Single leaf doors were fitted throughout for the first time on tube stock; these had been used also on the D78 District Line trains which we will shortly examine, and

both types had the same door opening button arrangement. However, their lesser width combined with the inevitable delay caused by passengers waiting for the 'door enable' light to illuminate before being able to open their door, means that such a format cannot perform as well as traditional double doors in being able to load and unload passengers in crush loaded conditions on central area platforms. It is for these reasons that they will almost certainly never re-appear in any future tube train development. Ten years further on from the Piccadilly Line trains, these trains had lost all of the subtly pleasing aesthetic features that had made the 1973 Stock so special. Design Research Unit had not been asked either to comment on or to influence the design in any way. The interior design had many faults including an inappropriate re-use of the colours contained in the orange, yellow, mustard and brown seating moquette.

Whereas the design solution for the D Stock trains was to use this moquette in pleasing harmony with the chosen interior colours of oatmeal, orange and brown, the mistake was made to use the mustard tone as a major feature colour in the 1983 Stock! This was applied indiscriminately to the draughtscreens, the backs of the transverse

Last of the line! What would become the very last coachbuilt train type built for London Underground. The sharp edged corner treatment of the cab was completely at odds with the much softer detailing of the rest of the vehicle.

The interior design and colour scheme which engendered such a strong negative reaction from the LT Design Committee. The excessive use of mustard (turmeric) colour and the overall mediocrity of the detailing provoked the response, fully endorsed by the LT Board, that henceforth design consultants must be involved in the development of any new train. The second and third interior views on this spread were taken later in life when a revised design of handgrip had been fitted.

seats, the door and window facings and the entire ends of the car with particularly unfortunate results. If one had had a rather over-indulgent weekend, the moment of truth of entering this overbright and brassy interior on a Monday morning made one not only long for the comforting, cosseting gentility of the 1938 Stock's interior but was also a stark reminder of how far the high standards of Underground rolling stock interior design had been allowed to slip!

Apart from the unfortunate choice of colours the general level of detailing was also very poor; the only worthwhile innovation being the specification of a continuous band of luminaires on each side running in an unbroken line from one car end to the other over all of the doors. Because these were inadequately sealed against tunnel dust as a consequence of their design and construction, even these were replaced by time honoured recessed bare tubes when a further order was placed in late 1986 for a further 16½ trains to augment the service. The first few cars from the initial order

had an additional interesting innovation in that the sloping grabpoles entering the draughtscreens by the double doors were continued over the doors in a single cranked hoop design. Unfortunately this simple and stylish configuration was soon replaced by separating out both elements and employing the traditional solution of a separate handrail over the doors.

The rest of the car interiors ignored nearly all of the passenger orientated design features which had been developed on tube trains over nearly 50 years! The transverse seat backs had no inviting shape or form to them, being totally sharp edged and rectilinear and the bitty, overcomplicated shape of the ceiling fan housings was even uglier than on 1973 Tube Stock. There was an over-abundance of fixing screws to be seen throughout the car. These secured not only all of the interior body panelwork but also many individual trim pieces and sections; more than could be seen on any other design of Underground train. Generally these can be reduced by skilful attention to detailing at the design stage to ensure that all sub-assemblies and components can be readily and conveniently assembled during manufacture within the tolerances imposed in the manufacture of the carbody, but the 1983 Stock shows that many expedient decisions were taken.

Not only does the integrity of the final appearance suffer when this happens but the interior is put at risk by some of the

organisation's 'customers' who carry Phillips screwdrivers on their person and are bent on mischief! However, to end on a fairly positive note, there was some thought given to the cleanability of the stock and past practice was continued by the use of angled wooden trim pieces around the bases of seat risers and draughtscreens.

From a historical perspective it is interesting to note that these trains would be the last to be built for the Underground with two intrinsic features dating right back to the earliest days of this century – incorporated in the first multiple-unit tube cars built in 1903 for the Central London Railway (the same year that the Wright Brothers first flew at Kittyhawk!). They were the grooved maplewood flooring and the straphangers individually suspended from the ceiling. We will see in a later chapter how these were subsequently to be designed out for reasons of fire safety in the case of the first and overcoming vandalism in the case of the second.

Finally, two significant facts about these trains. First of all, on the very day that they first entered service, 2nd May 1984, it was announced that three different prototype trains for new Central Line stock had been ordered in order to investigate, develop and test many ground-breaking alternative solutions. These were to lead to a completely new concept in tube rolling stock design.

Secondly, these trains would share a similar destiny with the Central London's original loco hauled trains and the Watford Joint Stock vehicles from the First World War period in having an extremely short operational life on the Underground system. Scrapping of the 1983 Mark 1 vehicles had already commenced in earnest in the middle of 1998, to make way for the brand new trains that had been built for the Jubilee Line and its extension (see later chapter). Generally no-one was sorry to see them go because, apart from their poor aesthetic design and the operational difficulties caused by the single leaf doors, there had always been a number of mechanical problems with the bogies; furthermore the trains also had ongoing electrical problems which the line was continually having to 'fix'. However it is a different story with the Mark 2s, which will stay but in a completely revised form. A considerable amount of planning and development time was spent at the end of the 1990s to investigate how at least fifteen trains could be converted to the same design standards as those of refurbished 1973 stock for further service on the Piccadilly Line. This was originally proposed to be the most extensive refurbishment programme ever undertaken because a return to double doorways was envisaged as part of the scope of works, but a decision was later made to retain the single leaf doors after all.

The interior treatment borrowed heavily from the surface D Stock cars, but went sadly wrong along the way. The ugly ventilation fan housings were the last straw! Both stocks used the same moquette pattern of 'stacked bricks' design in orange, yellow, mustard and brown; this was inherited from an aborted limited stop express LT bus project which was to have been painted yellow all over. When this bus project was cancelled, this moquette had already been developed and it was looking for a new home. This turned out to be the later examples of LT's rear-engined DMS double-decker bus fleet and any available design of train that was on the stocks that could use it.

SURFACE STOCK TRAINS

In May 1968 an order was placed with Metro-Cammell Limited for a total of 212 cars to make up thirty-five 6-car trains plus one spare 2-car unit. The first train of what became known as C69 Stock went into service in the autumn of 1970 and all of them were in service by the end of 1971. Their delivery enabled the remaining CO/CP vehicles to be transferred to the District Line, allowing all the remaining Q Stock to be scrapped. A further order of eleven 6-car trains was later made to replace those trains of CO/CP Stock needed to operate the Wimbledon–Edgware Road service of the District Line. Delivery started in mid-1977 and they became known as C77 Stock.

Although Design Research Unit had, as we have seen, very positively influenced the appearance of all of the tube trains developed during this period, their LT Design Survey Report of June 1971 indicates that they were neither consulted on the exterior or the interior design of C Stock. Their report quotes as follows: "The exterior of the new Circle and Hammersmith & City Lines stock is retrogressive in its design as it re-establishes the low-browed look in spite of the success of the high forehead of Victoria Line driving cabs." They urged that a more radical approach to the design of rolling stock was needed for the future. "At present, design initiation is largely the result of collaboration between London Transport and Metropolitan-Cammell engineers. Design proposals for the exterior form and interior treatment are submitted to the Design Panel when these have virtually reached finality and only minor modifications can then be proposed. This was the case when the Victoria Line stock was being designed; submission was made at an even later stage in respect of the new Piccadilly Line stock; the Design Panel was not consulted at all on the Circle, Hammersmith & City Line trains apart from being invited to comment on the colour of the interior(!). At this late stage any proposed modification is castigated as increasing cost unnecessarily."

This was obviously a very sad state of affairs which had been allowed to develop by an organisation whose predecessors had done so much to make London Transport a world recognised leader in the application of the highest standards of design for rolling stock. The Design Panel clearly had no teeth at the time; the significance of the major contributions already made by both the Design Panel and the DRU had not been recognised and as a result they had been ignored. This was particularly surprising when the outstanding and highly influential work done by DRU for British Railways throughout the 1960s (which became the model for other railway companies all over the world to follow) is taken into consideration.

A C69 Stock train when new in June 1970. It is hard to believe that this design represented 33 years of design *advance* over the O, P and Q stocks of 1937! Somehow the only character that it exudes is one of being dull, stolid and workmanlike. The style and flair that its pre-war antecedents could demonstrate in abundance was now totally lacking!

Inset One very worthwhile development however was the powered side cab access door, specified for the first time on an Underground train.

The beetle-browed C Stock trains can best be described as being worthy and workmanlike but neither their original exterior nor interior design exhibited anything like the panache, individuality and careful attention to detail of their predecessors with flared sides. With four sets of doors per bodyside, they were conceived for mass movement because the majority of journeys on the lines which they serve are short distance and this number of doors per side allows for rapid exiting and entering.

They possessed operational features that pre-dated those of 1973 Tube Stock in that the train operator's cab door could be independently controlled with its own air supply. A 'selective close' facility enabled all but one pair of doors to be closed at terminal stations in cold weather. As originally fitted out, eight transverse seats were positioned between the draughtscreens which allowed increased standing accommodation. The then typical light blue laminated plastic surfaces trimmed with satin anodised extruded sections were used throughout and transverse bulkheads carried illuminated advertising panels, as on the 1967/1972 tube trains. The blue and green moquette harmonised well with the colour scheme.

The interior was never particularly distinguished even when new, but over the years it wore extremely badly. Aerowalk material covering the heaters peeled away, the illuminated advertisement frames were often empty and unilluminated, again showing the build up of dust, and towards the end of the 1980s these trains were being particularly badly hit, both inside and outside, by the graffiti menace. This made the trains look particularly hostile and threatening. There was also a major problem with the chosen seat layout which had never been anticipated at the design stage. The sets of transverse seats, hemmed in on either side by draughtscreens, produced an environment of individual cells. As a result of this layout, women in particular were at risk in a lightly loaded train travelling at off peak hours because fellow travellers at the other end of the car could see nothing (see illustration above). The refurbishment process that we will examine in a later chapter enabled these unfortunate interiors to be totally redesigned.

Photograph of the interior when new. The transverse bulkheads carrying illuminated advertisement panels would progressively become an eyesore as well as a maintenance headache in the years to come, due to dust accumulating in the corners and a mixture of panels, some lit and others not. It was on this stock that the blue and green moquette made its first appearance and its colours accented the pale blue melamine laminate panelling of the interior that was trimmed with satin anodised aluminium extrusions and castings.

Being considered at the time of C Stock delivery was the use of glass fibre seating, seen here fitted experimentally to P Stock car 014082. The idea was not taken further.

143

Below Two views of the scale model which was produced by DRU in 1974 to define the design approach for London Transport and Metro-Cammell. This time around, the dated low-browed look of C Stock had been effectively replaced by a beautifully simple, elegant and well-proportioned face for these new trains. The sheer body sides and the single leaf doors, two very distinctive features of the trains, were already firmly established.

Bottom The partial length full size mock-up of D Stock photographed at Acton Works in 1976.

The D78 Stock trains for the District Line present a much happier story. These replaced the bulk of the line's CO/CP and R stocks between 1980 and 1983. Each train is made up of six cars and each vehicle is almost 60 feet in length. Passenger operated door opening buttons were fitted as was the selective close control feature to keep in the warmth while waiting at terminal stations in cold weather.

As we have seen, passenger operated doors were not a new idea, having been first introduced in 1936. Because of their unreliability they were not in use for long before the war finally put paid to them. During the 1950s they were in use for somewhat longer (ten years on the Bakerloo) but again, the feature was not long lived.

Design Research Unit's 1971 London Transport Design Survey report must have had some impact within the organisation because this time DRU did play a role in shaping the appearance of these trains; however they were only able to influence the external design. This they did very effectively because the cab front is a worthy companion to the 1973 Stock cab; they are both commendably clean, simple and well proportioned. A young German industrial designer, Jurgen Greubel, was working for DRU throughout 1974 and he prepared a series of layouts in the middle of that year as well as a scale model in order to assist Metro-Cammell in defining the appearance. The sheer bodysides, the proportions of all of the windows and the single leaf doors of the final train are all there to be seen in his work. Jurgen had taken one year out from working for Dieter Rams, the renowned German industrial designer who had developed over the years the unique design strategy of the world famous Braun

A visual prepared by DRU in 1974 of their rolling stock proposal for the new Hong Kong Mass Transit Railway System, for which they had been appointed overall design consultants. The sheer carbody sides would prove to be very similar on the D Stock.

electrical products, and he returned to work for him again following his stay in London.

Although these trains are sometimes irreverently described within London Underground as 'looking like a sixties tower block on its side', the external detailing of the aluminium bodywork mounted on its aluminium underframe is very simple yet reveals some very subtle niceties. Since these cars were longer than their predecessors, they had to be narrower in order to negotiate all of the curves on the line. The bodies were built as wide as possible at floor level but needed to be narrower towards the roof. The sides could have been waisted as previous designs but a decision was taken by the engineers and designers at Acton Works this time to have totally flat sides which sloped in at a slight angle.

These trains were developed and built at Washwood Heath at the same time as Metro-Cammell were building the MTRC vehicles for the then new Hong Kong Metro, and they share many similarities in construction and design. This is not surprising since Design Research Unit were also the design consultants for these trains and they played a major role in developing their design.

Again they were not asked to contribute any thoughts and ideas for the interior design, yet this was and remains to this day an extremely competent solution. It very successfully demonstrates all of the required attributes of being warm, bright, friendly and inviting. In contrast to the 1983 Tube Stock, the moquette material was used in pleasing harmony with the slightly patterned oatmeal coloured laminated panels that were pleasingly accented by the now somewhat dated late seventies fashionable colours of orange and brown. Nevertheless, the contrast between the interior of these trains and the grey, murky ambience of C69/77 Stock in their original form was very real in terms of greatly enhanced passenger appeal. The proof of the pudding was that when passengers had the choice of which train type to use, the newer trains would often be chosen even if this meant a longer wait before departure! Passenger preferences were also affected by the appalling ride of C Stock trains and the poor effect on passengers caused by having only three motor cars (which accentuated the effect of throwing people about when the trains went over current rail gaps with the motors under load). D Stock was much better in this regard.

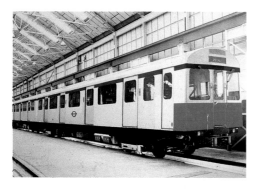

This page Five alternative ideas to develop a dedicated District Line identity for the new trains. The asymmetrically positioned two vertical bands of green shown at the foot of the page is a particularly late 1970s design solution.

Opposite page above A complete train of D Stock photographed in 1978 during its first days in service on the District Line.

Opposite page below Interior of D Stock showing the open airy ambience and excellent through car visibility. This view was taken in the mid-1990s and still presents a modern appearance. Only minor alterations have been made since new, including the installation of opening sections on the single glazed windows half way along the car and the painting of the end door brown instead of orange. The hand grips on the transverse seats were also added after delivery.

The depth of the draughtscreen glazing was commendably low, which not only contributed to the open aspect and airiness of each car but also provided good visibility from one car end to the other; a positive security feature. The lighting tubes were partially recessed within two simple troughs which ran along the car's entire length and these gave effective illumination to all parts of the car. Indeed, unlike all of its contemporaries, both tube and surface, the interior demonstrated a pleasing overall integration of all the design elements, notably the extruded aluminium ventilation grilles, the lighting troughs and the framing of line diagrams and advertisements. Finally, unlike 1983 Tube Stock, visible fixing details were kept to a minimum and any that did show were discreetly handled. Indeed the whole car's interior still stands up today as an object lesson in how to design and detail an interior which effectively deals with all of the manufacturing tolerance issues.

Before the trains went into service, there were some interesting attempts to develop a dedicated District Line identity by applying either one or two shades of green onto the satin aluminium bodywork. All of these ideas came to nothing and the trains went into service with their bodywork completely unadorned except for the red panel applied to the lower part of the cab.

CHAPTER SIX

The years 1984 to 1992

Below and top opposite The earliest sketches for 'designer' tube trains were produced by DCA around the middle of 1982. DCA were initially encouraged by London Underground's development engineer Roger Aylward to investigate really radical solutions of which the extensive glazing was but one. At these early stages it is fair to say that DCA did not thoroughly assess production feasibility, cost and safety aspects; they were not asked to.

Bottom opposite Not quite so radical! This sketch features a profiled nose with continuous flush tinted glazing.

Particularly in the light of the disappointing design of the C69/77 Stock, the following recommendations had been made by Design Research Unit in 1971 in their London Transport Design Survey regarding a future strategy for rail vehicle design. They said:

"We recommend collaboration between mechanical engineers and industrial designers in the design of new rolling stock and the consideration of their joint proposals by the Design Panel at a stage when changes to existing practice can still be accepted without 'modifications' involving extra expense. The Design Panel should be strengthened and be given clear authority on all design aspects of the London Transport undertaking which significantly affect the relationship between the travelling public and the Executive. A new attitude to total design is now necessary. This will require central direction of all design manifestations of London Transport."

A full eleven years later, these recommendations were acted upon when Roger Hughes joined London Transport as the first in-house Industrial Design Manager. His appointment augmented the Architects Department which then became the Department of Architecture and Design under W. D. C. (Donald) Hall. Roger's appointment was very timely because the design of replacement stock for the Central Line was now a burning issue.

We have seen how the development of tube train design since 1938 had been evolutionary rather than revolutionary, with the exception of one or two major technical changes, i.e. automatic train operation rheostatic braking on 1967 Stock and the longer cars of 1973 Stock which incorporated a modern brake control system. The principal components, the car bodies and the traction control system had changed very little in comparison with designs elsewhere in the world with no major step changes being introduced. This certainly had a lot to do with the need to provide compatibility with existing rolling stock, signalling systems and maintenance requirements; but in addition the existing designs had always fairly readily met the required reliability standards.

It was announced in May 1984 that prototype tube trains would be ordered to test a number of new design features in preparation for the ordering of brand new stock for the Central Line, and also to obtain comparisons between available manufacturers and the equipment they offered.

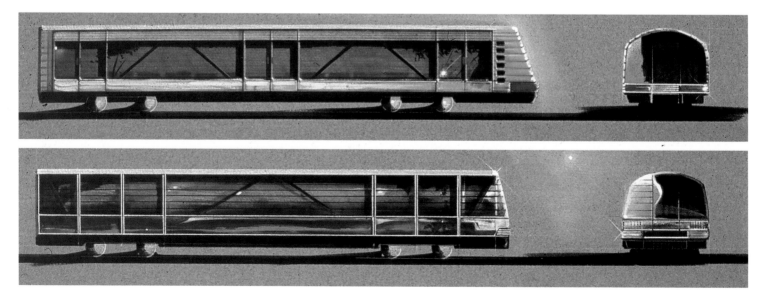

An early scale model. The soft *horsecollar* type nose recalls the treatment used on the later Danish ICE trains.

David Carter CBE, RDI.

Four more early study models that were produced for an initial progress meeting with London Underground engineers.

Financially, 12 cars were affordable and this number corresponded to three 4-car trains, each made up of two 2-car units. Four companies were invited to put in bids, these being British Rail Engineering Limited (BREL), Metro-Cammell, CIMT of France and the German Wagon Union in Berlin. The UK firms were successful, BREL being contracted to build one train and Metro-Cammell two. Power equipment was ordered from Brush and GEC in the UK and from Brown Boveri of Germany.

There clearly was also a great design opportunity to seize and London Transport's Department of Architecture and Design researched several UK Industrial Design Consultancies during the middle of 1982 with a view to choosing one company to work with the engineers at Acton right from the project's inception. DCA Design Consultants were chosen and they were invited to submit their first stage proposals in October 1982, their remit being to work on all of the ergonomic and visual aspects of the new trains. One of the contributing factors to their being chosen was their capability to build full size mock-ups at their Wedgenock facility in Warwick.

DCA was founded by David Carter CBE, the eminent British industrial designer, in the late 1950s and his vision was such that his company was the first UK industrial design consultancy to also employ both mechanical and electronic engineers to give his clients an all embracing in-depth service.

British Rail had done much pioneering work on their prototype APT tilting train in the late 1970s using loadbearing extruded aluminium body sections which were then welded together. There were also parallel developments in France, Germany and Switzerland with this construction technique. These developments were of interest to the Underground's rolling stock engineers because post-war tube cars, although sheathed in aluminium, had continued to use steel underframes. The reason for this was that in order to achieve the equivalent stiffness in aluminium, structural members would be required of such considerable depth that access to equipment would be greatly impeded. Therefore the use of wide extrusions welded together offered a solution if the whole bodyside could be made loadbearing. In this way a lighter structure could be provided which could also substantially reduce energy consumption.

The technical specification was developed jointly by Keith Ware, then Senior Design Engineer and Roger Aylward, the development engineer on the project. They both wholly supported and actively encouraged DCA's involvement. As well as exploiting all of the design possibilities that the extruded aluminium welded construction could offer, technical innovations would also be incorporated such as air suspension, motors on all axles, pressurised ventilation for the passenger saloon areas and electronic 'thyristor' control of the operating current. On some cars, steered bogies and motor mounted disc brakes would also be tried.

Underground procurement policy was undergoing a major change at that time. Traditionally LUL had retained overall project management for each train contract and would order the vehicles and traction equipment separately, being then responsible for bringing everything together at the manufacturer's works.

But from now on the manufacturer would design and build the train against a performance specification, and to provide a competitive element more than one manufacturer had to be involved in the process. DCA's initial brief was remarkably general and they were encouraged to explore all possibilities including swoopy front ends (their parlance of the time), larger windows and different styles of seating. At the outset even wide-access 'gull-wing' saloon doors, fully glazed sides and doors over a structural skeleton, articulated cars and cars with no seats at all were briefly considered. However after a couple of weeks into the project, the main 'givens' were established such as the need to strengthen the structure around the door pillars of an extruded aluminium monocoque bodyshell and replacing the time-honoured strap hangers with something better.

Discussions were also held around the possibility of introducing smaller wheels which would not intrude into the floor space of the saloons but it was soon conceded by Roger Aylward that the required materials and braking technology were not sufficiently developed. From that point on, the continuing need for large wheels would dictate the position of the longitudinal seats and the doors. Very early coloured sketches show not only the earliest thoughts for a profiled front (soon to be abandoned because of the limitations that these pose on making up train formations) but also two of the main design features that would find their way onto the trains as finally built. These were the externally hung doors operated by an overhead linear door operator (then thought necessary because of the engineering design constraints imposed by extruded aluminium bodywork) and large sealed panoramic windows to allow standing passengers in seat bays to see out readily to read station names. At last the visionary aspirations of the 1949 'sunshine' car were finally to appear on Underground trains almost 40 years later!

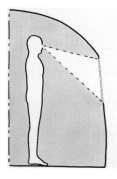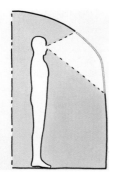

Above An interesting comparative sketch produced by DCA showing the vastly superior field of view for standing passengers that the panoramic windows achieved. William Graff-Baker's visionary ideas from 1949 finally resurface over three decades later!

Right One of the few sketches that were produced early on in the project (by Martin Pemberton) showing the now typical *flying buttress* ceiling treatment of cars built from welded aluminium extrusions. This is necessary to achieve the required torsional rigidity around the large door apertures.

Below Two sketches exploring the impact of completely flat, vertical cab fronts.

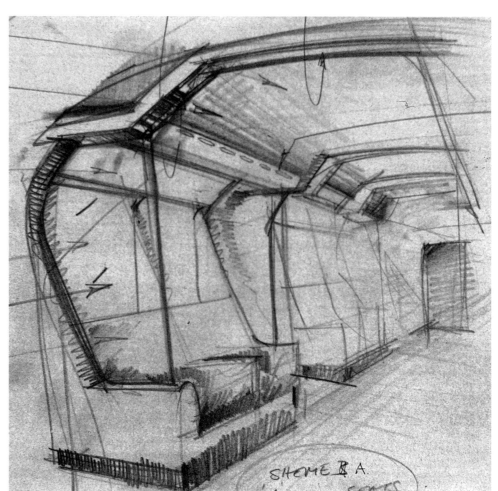

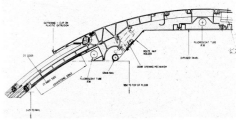

DCA worked in three dimensions right from the very start preparing only a few sketches and plan drawings along the way. 'Flying buttresses' would be necessary to maintain torsional stiffness around the large door apertures and would subsequently characterise the internal appearance of all the prototype and ensuing production trains built from welded aluminium extrusions.

In order to make sense of all the ideas coming forward, David Carter decided to present them to London Underground in the form of three stand-alone concepts. Although some of the ideas were more promising and developed than others, they were all spread across three designs in what became the Red, Green and Blue trains. They were only thus colour coded to avoid confusion, not because it was thought that green and blue was a good idea for a Central Line colour scheme. Martin Pemberton was given the job of developing the Green train, Hans Petersen the Red train and Michael Groves worked closely with David Carter on the Blue train, the front end of which being also designed by Hans.

Martin Pemberton stated that: "One of the reasons I was asked to work on the project was because I was the only bona fide interior designer on the staff. Having no prior experience of trains my own starting point was to take a very architectural approach. This resulted in the hooped ribs down the length of the car which compartmentalised the seating bays, without closing them in, and gave a vaulted appearance to the ceiling. The intention was to make the interiors look bigger and brighter and to this end the vaulting gave a sense of scale and importance to the saloons – as it does in a church – and the ribs were painted as a feature with the in-fill panels left as a light colour. The forms of the seats and grab rails were then integrated within this framework in a very ordered way as opposed to the previous 'plant-on' approach."

Above left The first full size complete cross-sectional mock-up that was built, which allowed both of the designers assigned to the project to simultaneously develop their ideas on each side.

Above Drawing and production of a detailed mock-up to test the light output of concealed fluorescent tubes and also the ergonomic requirements for semi-shrouded continuous handrails.

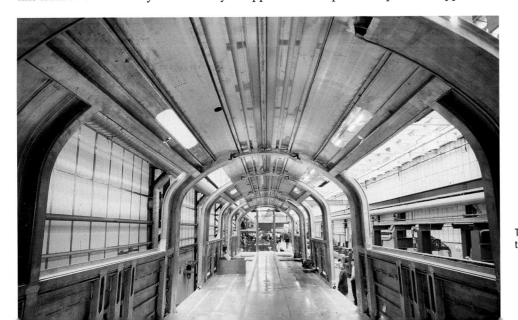

The extruded aluminium body shell of prototype train A at Metro-Cammell's Washwood Heath factory.

Above The three one-tenth scale models with their exterior styling details finally resolved.

Below David Carter's external designs for the Red, Blue and Green trains.

When Metro-Cammell won the bid to build the Red and Green trains (which were close variations on a theme) it was decided to build three full size interior mock-ups consisting of a car end and the first seating bay. These were extremely convincing in visual terms and were also very useful when it came to testing the ergonomics and trying out colour schemes and fabric patterns. Some issues that surfaced during this stage were the concept of putting perch seats on the car end equipment boxes and the need to avoid head or hand trapping features around grab rails and draughtscreens. It was also at this point that David Carter started to experiment with setting back the centre longitudinal seat bays on the Blue train version (which was to be built by the then British Rail Engineering Limited). These would make a reappearance on the final production trains of 1992 stock.

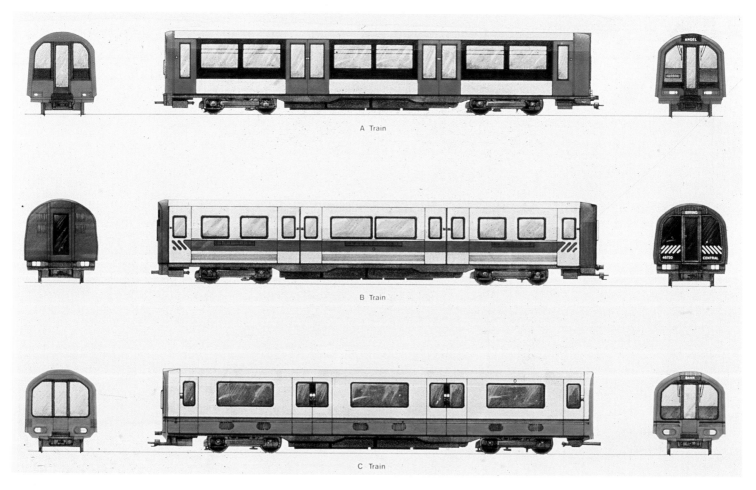

A Train

B Train

C Train

There were many firsts fitted on all three trains. New materials and fresh design ideas were exploited as well as the incorporation of some novel and important safety and convenience features for passengers.

At last there was a break from the grooved maple wood flooring after an eighty year span! This was replaced by continuous rubberised flooring material with repeating embossed discs, a material which was very popular at the time in architectural applications. In the past, other non-wood floors had been tried but had been felt to be a poor substitute for maple. A substantial amount of development work was later carried out on flooring materials following the King's Cross fire disaster in 1987 (see later chapter), to specify materials that would comply with enhanced fire safety standards. This would render this embossed material obsolete.

Dot matrix destination indicator panels and digitised voice announcements giving passengers visual and audible information about the next station and the ultimate destination were fitted, the dot matrix units being positioned over the inter-car connection doors.

All the cars were also equipped with passenger emergency alarm buttons that sounded a warning in the cab initially rather than applying the brakes. The train operator could then use public address to speak only to the car where the alarm push-button had been operated, and the passengers could reply by microphones in the car.

Passenger door open push buttons were incorporated into the door leaves themselves and additionally door close buttons were provided for passenger use. Audible tones signalled the initiation of the door open and close cycles. Inspired by the fast rewind symbol on his new stereo system, Martin Pemberton designed a door button graphic to put on the mock-ups which has since become almost an industry standard.

Above and below left The three models of each interior that were built at one-twentieth scale as one car side, a mirror being used to create the illusion of a complete interior.

Bottom The attractive detailing of the green variant.

Below The design of the passenger operated door open and door close buttons. These were the first time that the *fast rewind* symbols had been used to describe the direction of door travel.

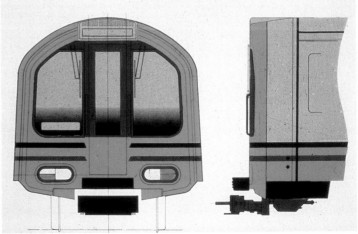

The one-tenth scale model of the Red train.

1. Metro-Cammell's Red 'A' train

The red and charcoal grey interior featured longitudinal seating with looped tubular armrests of circular section; these were fitted throughout each vehicle. Large car end windows were installed for the first time ever on a tube train, a feature which gave a more spacious feel resulting from good visibility from one car to the other and had major active security benefits for travellers. Virtually full depth glazing fitted to the inter-car connecting doors further reinforced the feeling of airiness at each car end and the perception of safer travel.

Each six unit seat bay was defined by a continuous red grabpole/handrail hoop treatment which also enclosed the bottom of the seating. The lower solid supporting members of the deeply glazed draughtscreens neatly echoed the bend radii of this tubular 'frame', resulting in an integrated seat module which in turn had a strong visual relationship with the two curved high level windows behind. These followed the bodyside curve into the roof line, although they started at a higher level than in existing tube stock types. Grab handles were recessed into the door surrounds themselves rather than being treated as an 'add-on' and the lighting was effected by shrouding the tubes to give a more relaxed, less stark ambience.

Right The 'A' train interior mock-up. The shrouding to the fluorescent lighting tubes softened the interior. However, it was inevitably the case that more tubes were required to achieve a similar level of lighting to that on earlier train types.

A feature that was not successful was that the car line diagrams were positioned at the eye level of a seated passenger of average height on a horizontal bar which bisected the large windows at their half-way point. This position nullified to a considerable degree the up to date visual impact which the large curved windows gave when inside the car. Furthermore there was a perceived problem in passengers being able to read platform signs clearly when standing in the seating bay zones. The designer's idea was that in addition to providing an aid for passengers to get in and out of their seats the rail would be able to contain the necessary equipment for a route map illuminated to show the next or present station.

The photographs opposite and above show the application of the large areas of satin black, accented by the red cab front and the red doors to produce a very attractive colour scheme which positively expressed the dramatic design changes from what had been seen before. The fully glazed interior inter-car door treatment was repeated on the cab access door and the deep cab windows were sprayed black on their lower inside faces. This effectively disguised the wall of the train operator's console and created a simple masked surround to the dot matrix car number indicator panel. The cab front capping the bodyside and roof extrusions was a large red painted glass reinforced phenolic moulding – a material also used on the other trains.

The production interior of the red train. Martin Pemberton is seen in a seat bay and the none too successful eye-level line diagrams are readily apparent in this view as is also the fact that the original design concept shown on the scale models was well translated.

Above The one-tenth scale model of the Blue train.

Below The mock-up of the Blue version. Note that the armrests are a variant of DRU's two-level design.

2. BREL's Blue 'B' train

This train was the most conventional of the three in structural terms. Internally, the most significant feature was the use of single transverse seats in a one plus one configuration in the centre bay which required high draughtscreens. The aim of this was to provide more space for standing passengers inside the car rather than around the door areas. In theory it would have been possible to accommodate two rows of standing passengers along each car. To meet this requirement there were vertical grabpoles between each pair of back to back seats with a continuous hand rail overhead. Inter-car connecting doors, wider than those on the 'A' and 'C' trains were also fitted which, together with their deeper glazing, contributed to a spacious 'open' car end; car end windows were however not fitted. Armrests were one-piece moulded versions of DRU's original two-tier design.

Because of the more traditional window layout, BREL had been able to use overhead ducts and vents for the pressure ventilation system. (In the Metro-Cammell cars the size of the windows prevented this and the air was blown into the saloon through grilles behind the seats. In all three trains, the heating and ventilation packs were installed beneath the seats.)

Externally the train had a very distinctive front end cap with a sharp edge radius running all around it; any thoughts of giving this particular vehicle a friendly, non-threatening front had been abandoned! BREL did however do an excellent job in accommodating the designers' wishes to blend the ventilation/destination panel fully into the exterior form; this was not achieved on either of the two other variants. The driver's door had the deepest glazing of all three cabs. It is interesting to compare the front of the 'B' train with the top illustration from the previously mentioned LT Design Survey Report of June 1971, entitled *Rolling stock design attitudes* and prepared some twelve years earlier (see page 133).

Above The interior of the Blue train, again a very faithful interpretation of the mock-up.

Left Production Blue train at Stanmore in trial service on the Jubilee Line.

The one-tenth scale model of the Green train.
Below The interior mock-up.

3. Metro-Cammell's Green 'C' train

This design was by far the most adventurous. It was the strongest in overall concept, the cleanest in terms of its detailing and also the most functional from the seating point of view. The sealed large single windows which wrapped upwards into the roof line dominated both the exterior and the interior design. Horizontal handrails were set into recesses in the ceiling coving and vertical grabpoles were raked at an adventurous angle away from passengers standing in the aisles. Armrests were cantilevered and echoed the form of the grabpoles with their tubular construction of lozenge section. Handholds were neatly recessed in the door surrounds.

The seats on this train were harder than on the other two as they had expanded foam cushions on a baseboard. (The seats in the other two trains all had sprung interiors with either natural hair/fibre or foam padding.) All three of them were, however, covered with a wool/nylon moquette blended 85/15 per cent, a departure from the 100 per cent wool material used traditionally. The bold notion indicated on the mock-up interior that enabled the shape of the seat back support moulding to be continued as perch seats in the stand back areas beside each door was also faithfully interpreted in the actual train. Lighting was provided by a series of central luminaires (as on the 'B' train).

Externally this was certainly the most successful of all three, having that elusive ingredient that still maintained the individual style which characterises London's tube trains, albeit in an entirely modern manner (this important cultural attribute was never really accomplished by the other two). This had a lot to do with the softer detailing of the elements and the manner in which the three cab windows were integrated by a black mask. The combined air intake/destination display module was originally intended to be flush fitting on all three trains. and not an 'applied box' However only the 'B' train retained this treatment into production.

Above The production interior.

The trains were presented to the press, user groups and London Underground staff at Woodford sidings in May 1987 and in-depth market research on all of their features was conducted in both static and mobile mode; these were all then assimilated and the best of them would form part of the specification for the definitive Central Line trains. The prototype trains went into passenger service on the Jubilee Line from May 1988 to August 1989 and an incomparable amount of useful data and operational experience was gleaned from them during this period. The complete exercise had cost less than 5 per cent of the projected cost of the all-new Central Line trains.

Below The particularly attractive 'face' of the production train which, more successfully than the other two versions, maintained the elusive unique character of a London tube train.

Unfortunately, some cars of the Red 'B' and Green 'C' train were badly damaged in a derailment towards the end of this period but even this regrettable episode taught London Underground a considerable amount about the damage that can be sustained by welded extruded aluminium bodies as distinct from coachbuilt ones.

Following extensive negotiations it was finally agreed in 1996 that one of the undamaged Green driving motor cars would escape the scrapman and be saved for posterity to become an LT Museum exhibit. We have already seen how landmark examples of tube train development such as the 1935 stream-lined stock and 1949 'sunshine' car have been lost forever with only photographs remaining of how they looked. It is gratifying that the important role that this car will have played in the development of today's and tomorrow's state of the art tube trains was recognised in time.

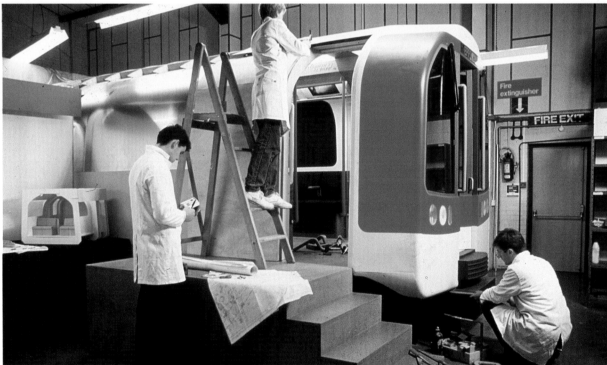

Top Scale model showing the original livery that was proposed by DCA for the 1992 Stock; off-white body shell with proportion of red on the cab front and with red doors.

Above Building the first mock-up at DCA's facility on the Wedgenock trading estate near Warwick.

The 1992 Central Line trains

Following a thorough analysis of the market research results on all the features of the prototype trains, DCA were then commissioned in late 1987 to develop a definitive design which was to include the best features from all three, together with any additional new ideas sparked off by the research.

The final train design essentially became a blend of the key features from the 'A' and 'C' prototypes. The bays of six longitudinal seats defined by the red up and over grabpoles/handrails came from the 'A' train and the generously proportioned sealed windows from the 'C' train. Large car end windows had also been shown to be an extremely popular feature from both the 'A' and the 'C' trains.

Another full size ergonomic test rig was developed and, out of this, two mock-ups were built by DCA to define the total exterior and interior design package. The first one was built as a design tool in late 1988 to demonstrate alternative ideas to enable a final design direction to be confirmed.

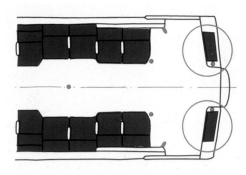

The first mock-up interior produced by DCA in late 1988 in its original form with alternative treatments of armrest shape and grabpole colours. A similar dot matrix destination indicator panel to that specified on the 1986 Stock prototypes is again positioned over the inter-car connecting doors (later, during the production development phase it was decided to remove this feature for cost reasons). The middle pair of seats set back 4 inches are also clearly apparent in this view and are shown also in the plan above.

The interior view shows the car end windows and perch seats, a choice of armrests looped or open (looped being chosen) and alternative colours for the grabpoles. The middle pair of the six seats in the outer bays was set back four inches to allow greater standing capacity in crush loaded trains; at this point there was a floor to ceiling grabpole in the centre. This layout eased a difficult movement around the pole with the other seats set forward due to the vent grilles. This feature was very much a personal initiative of David Carter himself and was made possible by the available underfloor space in this area which was freed up as a result of the geometry of the bogie travel underneath.

It would be found necessary to terminate the handrails above these two seats in order to allow passengers to get up and away from them safely, and extra perch seats were neatly positioned above equipment cabinets; these were located either side of the inter-connecting door at the non-cabbed ends of driving cars and both ends of cars without cabs. Some separate market research was carried out at this time to determine the pattern for the seat moquette and a version known as London Pride was the clear winner. Instead of the embossed rubberised flooring material of the prototypes, it was decided that the production trains would feature a completely flat floor made from a composite rubber material coloured dark grey, relieved by the inclusion of ivory and blue chips randomly dispersed within it.

The contract was awarded in 1989 to BREL at Derby (later to become ABB Transportation Limited and then ADtranz in 1995) who were given an order to produce eighty-five 8-car trains. A second full size mock-up was produced by DCA during the development programme in 1990 which was built to confirm ABB's interpretation of the design, and also to incorporate some recent corporate design decisions.

One of these was to apply the finally chosen corporate livery with red front and charcoal grey accenting around the cab windows, red doors and a lower blue accent panel. The positive results of the market research findings concerning the interior redesign of the 1967 Stock were so significant that it was decided that it made sense to apply the essentials of the same successful formula into the 1992 Stock as well. Thus the main interior body colour, ivory, was applied to the interior facings and DCA were briefed to develop a new moquette pattern that was bolder and more assertive. They came up with a very successful solution and this and the revised colourways were applied to the second mock-up.

Two of the moquette patterns designed by DCA that were market researched. The red and blue variant, called *London Pride* was the original winner but was later redesigned as a result of the more successful bolder pattern that was created for the seating of the Victoria Line's refurbished 1967 Stock, then also under development.

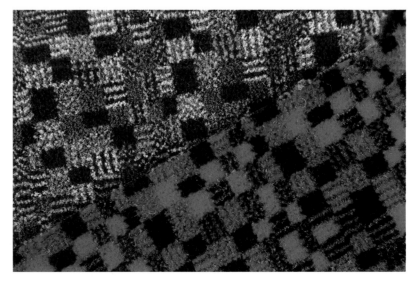

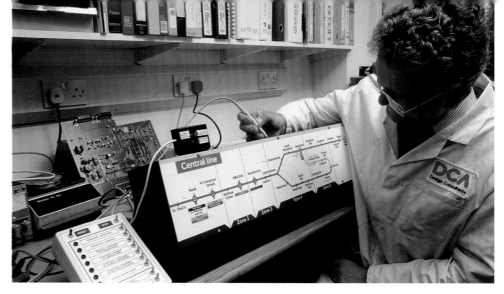

DCA, using their in-house electronic engineering capability, developed an illuminated bi-coloured LED system for the in-train line diagrams. Lights would identify the progress towards the next station on a route and then confirm it on arrival. Such a system is also in use within the Barcelona Metro vehicles but, unfortunately, it was another idea dropped to save cost.

In the production run, all of the car ends capping the extruded carbody assemblies, including the train operator's cab, were fabricated from large superformed aluminium sub-assemblies. This is a proprietary manufacturing technique where accurate aluminium pressings of high quality and finish, are created by the use of compressed air forming processes at high temperatures. This replaced the large glass reinforced phenolic mouldings which had been used on the prototypes. These had caused some concerns during the building of the prototypes because in some cases, tolerancing problems could create an imprecise match with the extruded bodyshell ends. These problems were inherent in this then relatively untried process but they have since been resolved.

The softer, more friendly face of the Green 1986 prototype was further developed and refined for the production vehicles, and the series of photos in this chapter from scale model, through full size mock-up to the final built product show how successfully the manufacturer interpreted the subtleties of the design. The large panoramic windows remain one of this train's most outstanding visual features and during the development process, it had been decided to increase the width of the double doors to 1664mm and the single doors to 832mm to optimise boarding and alighting times in the busiest central London stations. Each door leaf was now 150mm wider than was specified on the prototypes giving a clear door aperture of 1664mm.

Door open buttons were to be conveniently mounted on the doors themselves both inside and out, and these controls were repeated internally on the standback pillars together with accompanying door close buttons. All of these controls featured a tactile raised edge to guide the partially sighted.

Another first for London Underground was that the driving cab was designed and furnished with the same care and attention to detail as the passenger saloon areas. Although improvements in cab design had been made over the previous 30 years or so, the ergonomic design and layout of the driver's controls and instruments still often left much to be desired; the cabs were still often cramped and draughty with many of the operating controls awkwardly designed and positioned.

Addison Design Consultants were therefore commissioned to develop a totally new cab design since they had experienced designers in their team who had already developed the significant ergonomic improvements that can be seen in today's driving cabs of commercial vehicles. Traditionally a similar design attitude had existed in both road and rail vehicle industries, where all too often meeting the most basic requirements for the design of seating, and the shaping and positioning of controls and instruments, was considered to be good enough for the user. It is not that long ago that a truck driver had to make do with vertical and horizontal padded wooden seating boards for his overnight drive from Glasgow to London!

The environment of the production cab is, as a result, very comfortable, light and spacious with in-cab closed circuit colour monitors giving the train operator a full field of vision along any platform length on the line with all of the controls and instrumentation conveniently arranged. The redesigned fore and aft traction brake controller which is positioned at the right hand side of the driver's seat recalls the design approach that was installed in the cabs of the 1935 streamlined stock of over 60 years ago. Almost, but not quite, where we came in!

Inset top Final one-twentieth scale model produced by DCA.

Top A view of a completed production train showing how effectively the charcoal grey mask ties together all of the visual elements of the front of the cab.

Above Close-up of the passenger controlled door-open button on one of the interior door jambs.

Right Three views of the production interior showing its bright and spacious ambience.

Above Two views of the cab interior designed by Addison Design Consultants. The Siemens in-cab colour monitor which gives the train operator sightings along platform lengths can be seen mounted at the top right hand side.

Left Although the photograph shows a full set of armrests, these unfortunately would soon disappear in service due to vandalism. They were designed with 'frangible' joints, i.e. they would deliberately break away if a crush loaded car was involved in an accident, thus helping to prevent passenger injury. Sadly this design detail was discovered by the mentally challenged members of the public who promptly then kicked the armrests into oblivion! Although a redesigned version has been developed, they have not yet been fitted at the time of writing. The actual seat profile has also come under a certain amount of criticism from the comfort standpoint and although it does meet established ergonomic criteria for metro car seating, it is probably fair to say that the end result was not quite what the designers had originally intended. The design of the shrouded lighting treatment together with the continuous central luminaire can be traced right back to DCA's original concepts for the 1986 Stock.

CHAPTER SEVEN

The trains that never were

The 1990 funded design competition to develop concepts for brand new rolling stock for the Northern Line.

As we have previously seen from the early 1970s onward, the Northern Line had increasingly suffered from a bad press, particularly at the pen of the *Evening Standard*! The line in recent years had developed an unfortunate reputation for having the most delays and cancellations. Furthermore, travelling information given to passengers was often irritatingly out of date or no longer factual by the time that they received it. Its inheritance included the stations of the 1924 Morden extension and these had become very shabby and unkempt in appearance by this time.

The Northern had also paid the price for being the first to be equipped with dot matrix train describers. These, the first of the breed, became notorious for converting an indicated one minute wait into a five minute one! It had earlier been dubbed by both the media and the general public as 'the misery line', and when a specification for brand new rolling stock was being considered at the beginning of the decade to replace the time-honoured 1959 Stock, an exciting and innovative customer-led design approach was seen as a major factor that would convincingly re-establish the line's 'image' and its credibility to its users.

Six different Industrial Design consultancies were chosen to develop proposals against a brief, whose prime purpose was to stimulate the new ideas and thinking that was sought by London Underground's Northern Line development team. They did not want to stifle any fresh, original concepts at birth. Although cars with articulated bogies that could provide full open access through cars were originally considered as part of the specification, it was decided not to include this feature as part of the terms of reference because of the tight curves found on several of the line's platforms, particularly at Embankment (northbound).

Articulation trials had taken place back in 1971 when a 2-car unit of surviving flat fronted 1935 Stock (cars 10011 and 11011) were converted to assess the benefits of articulation for the new trains then being planned for the Heathrow extension of the Piccadilly Line. However, the benefits of articulation were not at that time considered to be sufficient to overcome the extra maintenance complications, so the idea was dropped. In this experiment, the two bodies had been cut back at their trailing ends and mounted on a single bogie but open through access was not incorporated.

Analysing the benefits that smaller than usual wheel sizes would bring to passenger interior volumes was however encouraged as was the concept of a train made up from cars with cabs fitted at both ends of the train only. This could then allow a profiled cab front to be developed since with in-cab CCTV for platform monitoring, only the cab door at the front and the rearmost passenger doors would have to be in the platform. Therefore the 'nose' of the train at both ends could be in the tunnel at station stops.

Let us look at the very interesting work that resulted.

Articulation trials on two withdrawn cars of 1935 Tube Stock in 1971.

Seymour-Powell Limited

Seymour-Powell developed a very bold and dramatic concept where the nose of the train would hinge up in the manner of a car hatchback which would then allow two streams of passengers to exit to the front in an emergency by passing either side of a centrally mounted driver's seat and console. In the drawing on the facing page (*centre right*) the arrows indicate the movement of the seat to get it out of the way in emergencies. With a TV screen in the centre of the control desk to monitor the platforms, and emergency egress to the sides, the central driving position certainly becomes a more realistic option.

Above and below The profiled nose of the Seymour-Powell proposal incorporated a 'car hatchback' in reverse to provide emergency exit points for two streams of people. The back of the train operator's seat would slide upwards with the squab then pushed down and under. This would enable the whole unit to be then slid forward to gain the maximum amount of space needed for the operation.

Below The two views of the interior show the designer's concept of chameleon seating. During the off-peak, all longitudinal seats would be locked in the down position. At the beginning of the peak rush hour periods, these would then be locked at terminus stations in the up position as shown to provide two banks of perch seats to allow 15 to 20 per cent more standing capacity. The three close-coupled vertical grabpoles in the centre could only have any relevance in this latter mode; with all of the seating locked 'down' they would create a real obstruction in a car of tube proportions.

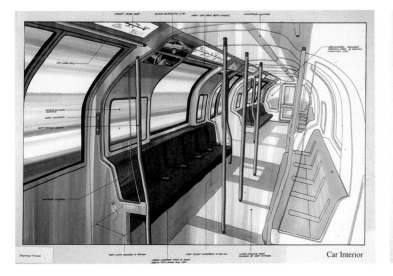

Car Interior

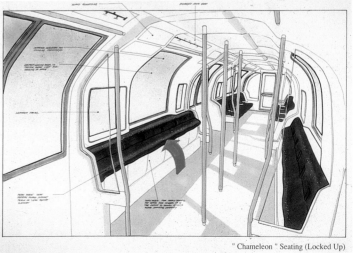

" Chameleon " Seating (Locked Up)

Exterior Design A Perspective

Above, right and below Perspective and elevational views of the Scheme 'A' car showing its three sets of double doors per bodyside.

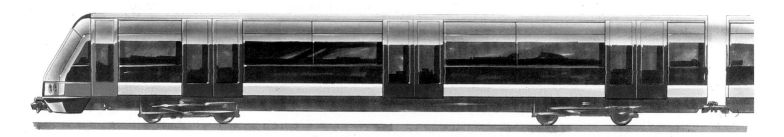

Design Triangle Limited

Three alternative schemes were prepared by Design Triangle with Scheme 'A' showing three sets of double doors per bodyside, a feature that would require a flat floor over the bogies, only possible with wheels of a smaller diameter than ever before. The Northern Line development team were interested in exploring the use of staggered doors with seating bays directly opposite, which formed part of Design Triangle's proposals. New York's subway system has proved that this layout can draw people away from the doorways, but perhaps it would be better employed on an all new design for Circle Line trains. Seated passengers would certainly be very vulnerable to horizontal driving rain or snow covering them in winter, not to mention drunks tumbling onto them! A very worthwhile idea however was that of splayed draught screens which, through their form, would 'lead' passengers towards the seats.

Top Diagram showing the seating bays directly opposite the staggered door layout, which was a feature of Scheme 'A'.

Below left View into the saloon of Scheme 'A' showing the curved draughtscreens to invite passengers into these areas with their integrated leaning posts.

Below right End door detail of Scheme 'A'.

Bottom Seat unit of Scheme 'A'.

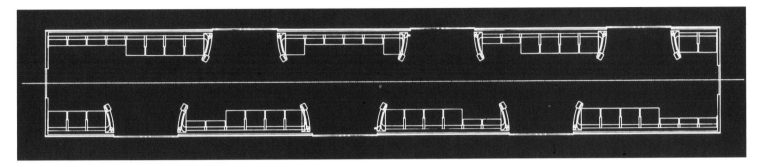

Interior Design A Saloon

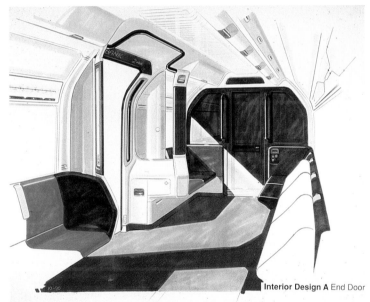

Interior Design A End Door

The cab design of Scheme 'A' used flat glass, while more expensive curved glass was proposed on schemes 'B' and 'C'. The distinctive 'fully glazed' appearance would, in fact, have been created by curving the windows on all three schemes into the roof. These would then meet solid infill panels painted in a glossy dark grey tone to simulate glass, which in turn aligned with the top of the doors.

The interior designs show real time information and destination displays in their most useful position above the doors, cantilevered seating to allow for easy cleaning underneath and where no packages could be secreted (this presupposes that all of the required operating equipment could be housed underneath the floor!) and generously padded and proportioned leaning posts, all integrated into a total interior concept.

A final design based on Scheme 'A', but produced some time later, shows an open inter-car connection (see page 177), rather than conventional doors at the ends of each car. Achieving such a clear through access in a tube stock vehicle would entail articulation or a great deal of development of the bogie and car end arrangements. One of the concerns on all tube lines (except the essentially straight Victoria Line where this feature may first appear on new stock) is that the lateral movement and end throw on reverse curves is very significant. This fact, coupled with the small scale of tube cars, makes it extremely difficult to preserve the required generous proportions of such an inter-car gangway.

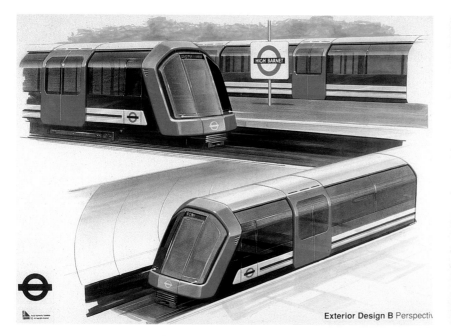

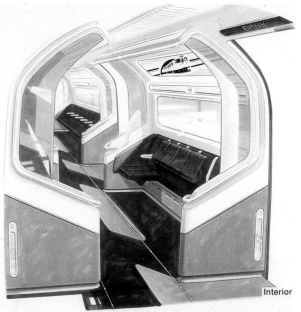

Exterior Design B Perspectiv

Interior

Exterior Design C Perspectiv

Top left Exterior perspective views of Scheme 'B' featuring curved glass panels for the cab windows.

Top right The saloon of Scheme 'B' showing grabpoles fully integrated into the draughtscreen edges.

Above left Exterior of Scheme 'C', just like a mini TGV! This was a somewhat inappropriate styling cue for a London Underground tube train.

Above right Door vestibule of Scheme 'C' showing the dot matrix destination and station indicator above the doors.

Right Interior of Scheme 'C'.

Below The proposal for an inter-car connection on Scheme 'A' which was produced by Design Triangle some two years later at London Underground's request (all of their previous offerings had conventional doors at the ends of each car).

Bottom left and right Design Triangle's proposals for the operator's cab and console.

Operators Cab

Operators Console

Below General view of the TDC interior and treatment of various details.

Below right Both of the proposed cab layouts.

Bottom The individual seating units, developed from their proposals for the refurbishment of 1973 Stock (see later chapter).

The Transport Design Consortium

Jones-Garrard Limited and Tilney Shane (part of the Transport Design Consortium) produced two concepts, one with the driver seated at the right hand side of the cab and one with a central driving position, emergency detrainment being effected on the latter version by just raising the large curved glass clamshell windscreen. The interiors were a development of the work which they had recently prepared for both the Victoria and Piccadilly stock refurbishments and thus continued and refined the same design concepts. For instance, the extremely open interior was a careful development of the former trains' unique character and the individual seat units were very similar to their redesigns for the 1973 Stock refurbishment. Their total design approach for exteriors, the interiors and the cabs is illustrated by the accompanying perspectives and drawings.

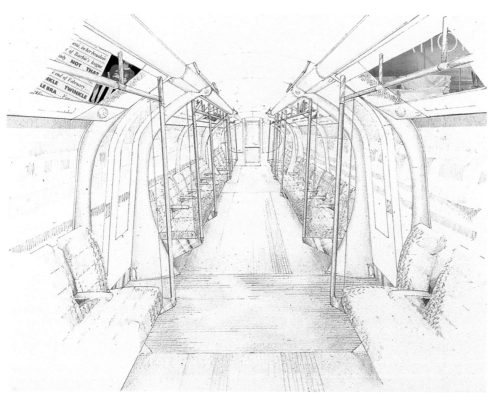

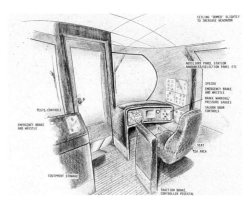

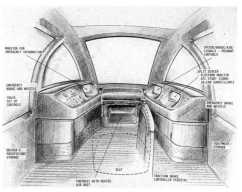

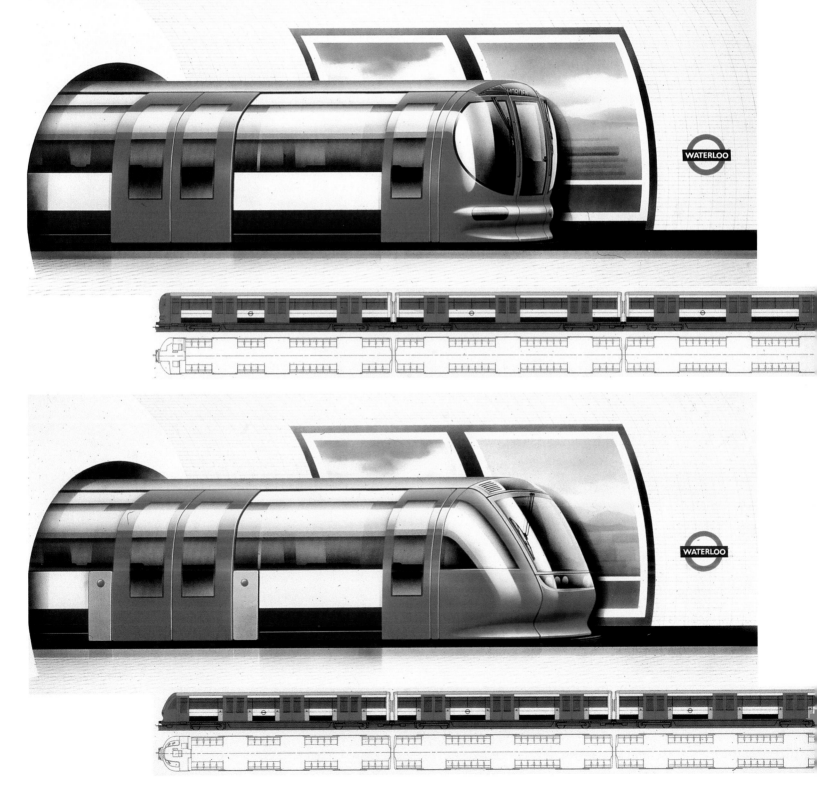

Below and inset Scheme 1: perspective showing Transport Design Consortium's 'primary design route'.

Bottom and inset Scheme 2: perspective of their 'concept design route' featuring a central driving position.

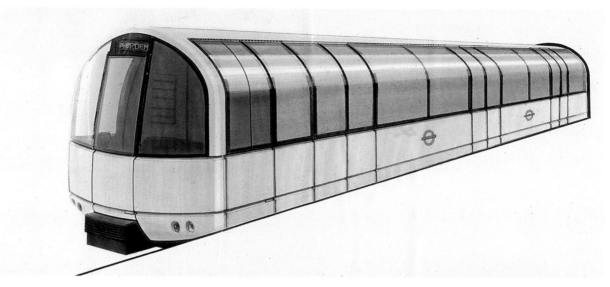

FM Design's understated proposal was a quite different approach in borrowing from the precise detailing seen in contemporary architecture. Door and saloon window glazing were fully flush giving the impression of a sheer expanse of glass. Sliding plug doors would have had to be specified to achieve such a styling.

FM Design Limited

This design house chose a totally different route, by re-interpreting the traditional form of an aluminium tube train by reinforcing the character of the tube in a manner that borrowed from the precise detailing seen in contemporary architecture. Door and passenger window glazing were fully integrated to give the impression of a sheer full expanse of glass, with vertical grooves and thicker window mullions delineating the door positions. It would be necessary to specify sliding plug doors to create the visual effect seen in the perspective and the elevation views. The form of the cab was subtly profiled, in the manner of some of Design Research Unit's work in the early 1970s.

Right The subtlely profiled cab design.

Far right The real time information display positioned in its most logical position; above the double doors when entering the car.

Below left and right Within the interior FM repeated two features that had been developed by the first two design companies; namely placing destination displays in their most logical and convenient position above the doors and also promoting the use of seats that could convert into a row of perches for peak service periods.

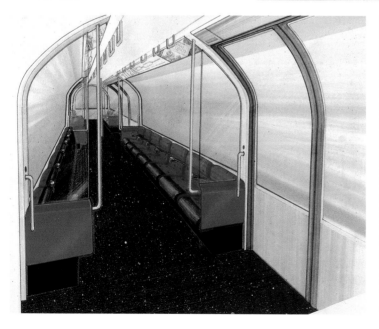

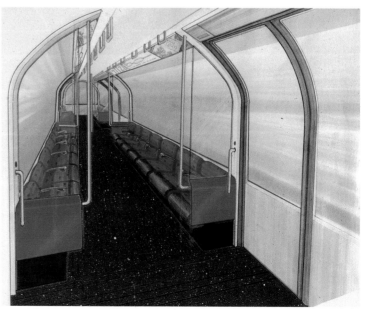

SIDE ELEVATION 1:50

Cre'Active Design Consultants

Cre'Active Design Consultants' stated object was to create a new tube stock with a personality of its own. The key building block of this work was to reflect the unique roundness of the tube tunnel within the design of the train itself. Thus the train received a unique round face, by enclosing the cab windows and centre cab door within a slightly convex disc which was set into the moulded cab front. Round running lights, cab side and door windows continued this theme of 'roundness'.

Since 70 per cent of departure stations on the Northern Line are from right hand platforms, including all the busy ones, they sensibly elected to put the train operator's

Above Study board showing two cars of a train in side elevation which shows the rationale behind the development of its unique appearance, intended to be quite different from that of a tram, bus or high speed train.

Below Development board showing how the design concept was evolved as well as details of the train operator's control console mounted to the right.

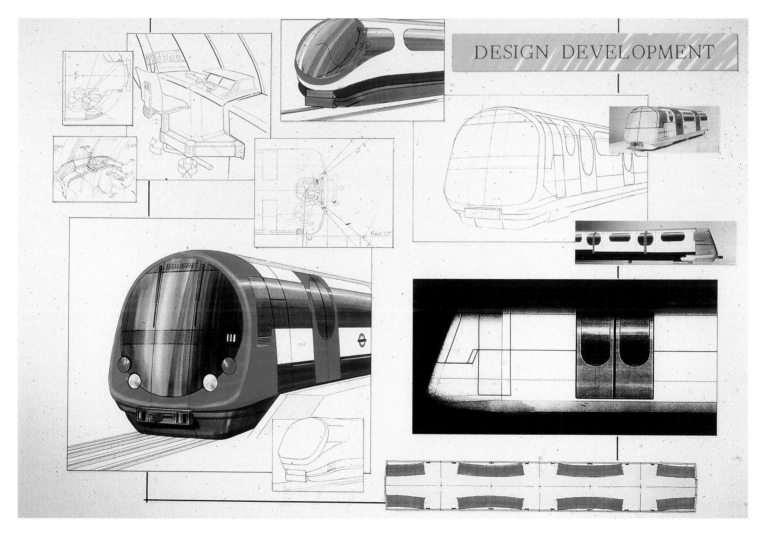

DESIGN DEVELOPMENT

Below The unique round face of the Cre'Active offering with the character of roundness also applied to the running lights, cab side and saloon door windows.

Facing page The *club-car* feel of the Cre'Active interior, this would certainly have promised a unique ambience for a London tube train! Plan views of the interior show lounge spaces, the seating units of which were common throughout the car. The resulting passenger flow patterns from this layout are shown as well as the location of the four different types of illumination which are detailed in the text. A very nice design for a London Underground tube train but at what price?

Interior of the Cre'Active cab.

control console on that side as well; in direct contrast to current Underground practice where the driver sits to the left for reasons which have been lost in history. Their cab was a particularly spacious one, with a high level of finish proposed to make it an attractive and desirable workplace.

Cre'Active really went to town with their interior, identifying the fact that the introduction of smaller wheels had created an opportunity for exploring new concepts for a more flexible usage of floor space. They therefore proposed to divide each car into three smaller saloons or lounges by means of a glass divider. Each lounge to consist of an integrated vestibule and seating area with easy access to the double doors, arguing that this design approach gave generous equipment space underneath. Seating capacity with this type of seating design was confirmed as 48 in a trailer car and 44 in a driving car.

To extend their unique club-car atmosphere which is so well captured in the air-brushed drawing and the accompanying plan views, four different types of illumination were proposed! First, indirect strip lighting reflecting off the ceiling with lightly perforated reflectors over the seating areas to give additional light and heighten the visual quality. Second and third, circular ceiling roses around the central grabpole and in the centre of each doorway to emphasise the grabpole positions and boost the ambient light in the doorways. Finally, uplighters were proposed either side of the glass partitions separating the lounges and the car ends to create a warm and inviting atmosphere, and downlighters located between the lounge sections to illuminate the gangway.

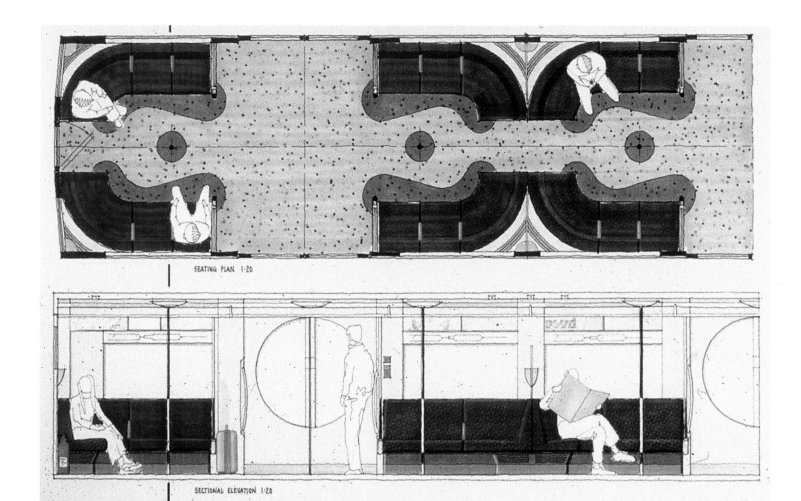

SEATING PLAN 1:20

SECTIONAL ELEVATION 1:20

INTERIOR

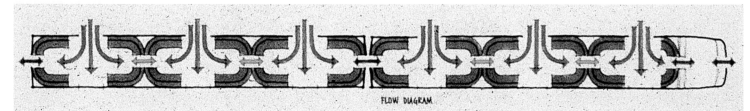

FLOW DIAGRAM

DCA Design Consultants Limited

This company also developed the theme of round door windows created by the meeting together of the two door leaves, but the front of their train had a pronounced angled horseshoe character, with the centre door and the cab windows neatly contained within it. DCA also examined staggered door layouts as a way to improve passenger circulation within the interior and two schemes were proposed – one with longitudinal seating and the other a return to sets of transverse seats for the longer journeys on the line; all of the seats having individually shaped backs to them. Tip up seats and deep standbacks were part of their proposals to create a versatile interior and carpeting (used successfully within the Metro cars in Washington since that

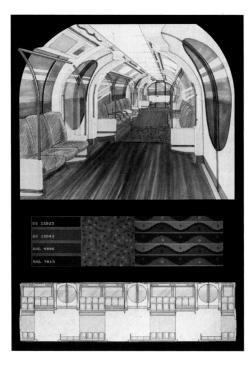
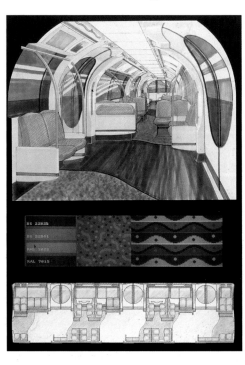

Above DCA's own solution for a profiled nose with its pronounced horseshoe character, neatly containing the cab access door and side windows. Like Cre'Active Design, they also proposed a double door scheme which created round windows when closed and a right hand side driving position.

Right Interior Scheme 'A' showing the staggered door layout, individual longitudinal seats and tip-up seats in the door vestibule area to maximise space in crush loaded conditions. Carpeting is specified in both the saloon areas and ends of cars.

Far right Interior of Scheme 'B' with transverse seating, a similar arrangement of tip up seats but a more interesting treatment for the carpeted floor areas.

system was opened) was imaginatively used to identify and separate the seating areas from those of the door vestibule. The two interior perspectives opposite graphically depict the arrangement of the staggered seating in relation to the doors. Animated computer generated visuals were also prepared for the competition; at the time this technique was still in its infancy. These still versions show the proposed interior through the open sliding doors and alternative suggestions for emergency detrainment through the cab door.

Top Computer generated exterior view with the doors open.

Above Computer generated views of three alternative suggestions for folding emergency detrainment steps.

Postscript to the competition

Following detailed review of all of these proposals, it was agreed that both Seymour-Powell and Design Triangle would be commissioned to embark on a further stage of design development which would also include the preparation of partial full size mock-ups. Unfortunately the necessary budget to carry out this Stage 2 work was never forthcoming and so the results of these exciting endevours never bore fruit.

It is very doubtful that London Underground will ever again hold such an adventurous and stimulating design competition involving such a large number of consultancies. In the future, a comprehensively worded specification will go out from them to rolling stock manufacturers for a new stock type and the manufacturer will commission their own industrial design consultancy to work with them to interpret correctly the customer's requirements. However, the competition resulted in a vast collection of ideas. Of course some of them were more practical than others, and no doubt many of them will crop up again in slightly modified forms in new rolling stock designs for many years to come.

All of this work was also, in the end, overtaken by events because new procurement policies, strongly supported by the Conservative Government, did pave the way for new trains to be ordered for the Northern Line. However this time they were to be very closely based on the new trains ordered from Metro-Cammell for the Jubilee Line and, for the first time ever, they would be leased to the organisation by the manufacturer who would also be responsible for all of the cleaning and maintenance issues as well.

CHAPTER EIGHT

The refurbishment era 1986-2000

Introduction

By the mid 1980s this was the unfortunate reality of how much of the fleet was presenting itself to its customers; the result of age and continual graffiti attack.

The same train design after refurbishment, the corporate colour scheme applied with graffiti resistant paint.

The various train refurbishment projects that started with the Victoria Line's 1967 Stock in 1988 and that ended with the District Line's D78 Stock, have been the most dramatic outward expression of London Underground's corporate culture change to both its customers and staff in recent years. The use of DCA Design Consultants on both the 1986 and 1992 stocks had already clearly demonstrated the significant added value that industrial design consultants can bring to a rolling stock design programme, provided that they are properly integrated with the in-house team and kept fully involved and informed with every stage of the design development process. It is these background factors that led to the continuing use of industrial design consultants to exploit every opportunity dramatically to reshape and improve the interior design of all of the trains involved in this extensive and far reaching programme.

In terms of the image of the train fleet as it was in 1987, it was apparent that there was a dichotomy between, on the one hand, the tremendous amount of time and effort being expended to create a new generation of tube trains and, on the other, the standard of presentation of the existing fleets to their passengers. The internal and external appearance of the various train types that had been built from the late fifties to the late seventies was increasingly suffering from not only the effects of wear and tear but also the results of sustained graffiti attack.

Their grey/blue interiors were all looking distinctly jaded and worn and this, together with the residual witness marks of graffiti, had made them appear hostile and threatening.

The then Marketing and Development Management of London Underground had already recognised these deficiencies by commissioning in early 1987 a series of sample boards from Messrs Haydon Williams International in order to investigate how interiors could be made more welcoming by developing new colour schemes and seat patterns. Since much of HWI's previous work had been undertaken for the motor industry, and since the private car was seen as the Underground's main competitor, it was perhaps natural that the ideas presented would be influenced by the then current patterns and colourways used in the interiors of private cars. It is for this reason that they did not seek to project a unique image for 'Metro' rail vehicles.

At the same time, the LUL Marketing Manager, Jeff Mills, also commissioned some work from the company's corporate identity consultants, Messrs Henrion Ludlow & Schmidt to develop concepts for a painted external livery for the trains in order to deal with the problem of graffiti attack on the outside of the trains. Some of the lines, notably the Metropolitan and Circle, were suffering badly from this problem but others such as the Piccadilly and Victoria Lines had remained relatively unscathed.

HLS's solution was to apply colour only to the cab front, the doors and the roof for those trains whose natural aluminium bodies still remained acceptable but to paint totally those trains where this was not the case. A silver toned light grey paint would ensure that a consistent appearance would prevail across the entire fleet. An A Stock train for the East London Line was the first to be painted in this style. Later HLS were to develop some alternative schemes, one of which featured a horizontal corporate blue panel that integrated the complete window line and they were also asked to investigate a line related approach. This was shortly after the

appointment of individual Line Managers. The former, though visually very successful was felt in some quarters to be too much like BR's Network SouthEast solution and the latter solutions were only partially successful. Unlike the DRU suggestions seventeen years before, to paint just the doors in line colour, these schemes maintained the horizontal window band approach. The Central, Metropolitan and District Line versions looked very attractive but the Northern and Bakerloo Line interpretations less so. Also there was a reluctance to paint doors in two colours whilst off the train because of potential alignment problems when refitted.

The tragic fire at King's Cross station in November 1987 happened at the same time as the initial stages of this work were developing. It at once not only radically changed every aspect of how the organisation would in future perform, but also suddenly provided the opportunity to improve and update dramatically the majority of the train fleet.

The King's Cross Fire

The rolling stock/modernisation programme grew out of some work that was already in hand to reassess all of the materials used from a fire safety standpoint but which was now given top priority. Following the King's Cross fire in 1987, a decision was taken to remove all of the materials in trains and within sub-surface stations that would give off smoke and toxic fumes in a fire and replace them with new ones. These would be fully compliant with newly created safety standards that would now become the most stringent in the world.

In the light of the organisation's previous attitudes to the interior design of vehicles, it is fair to say that had the disaster happened five years before it did, the materials within the trains would most probably have been replaced on a like for like basis, with the travelling public seeing little difference for the money expended.

However, there was now a new culture abroad due to the exciting results gained from the development of the 1986 prototype trains, and the fact that design management had just been made an integral part of London Underground Limited.

1. The 1967 Tube Stock Victoria Line trains

The first train type to be selected for refurbishment was a 1967 Victoria Line train, and the senior engineering manager on this project was Roger Aylward, the same man responsible for the 1986 stock programme. There was clearly an opportunity emerging to couple the replacement of materials such as fibreglass and melamine clad hardboard with other required engineering changes to improve the interiors radically. A transport design consultancy, Jones-Garrard, new to London Underground, was chosen to do the design work. They had just won an international competition to design the exterior of the Eurostar train and would work closely with Tilney Shane, interior design specialists on the project. A design brief was produced with the Design Manager working in conjunction with the designated engineering task manager to explore and agree all of the potential opportunities for change, together with detailed scope and costs of works.

This documentation was then ratified and regular fortnightly development meetings soon followed, attended by the design consultants, LUL's marketing and design management departments, engineering staff and line representatives.

The blue doors livery applied to four one-twentieth scale models of A Stock, D Stock, the 1986 green train and 1967 Stock.

The models painted with the horizontal corporate blue colour running through the window line.

The proposal using the appropriate individual line colours.

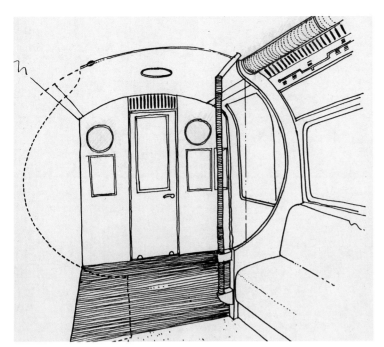 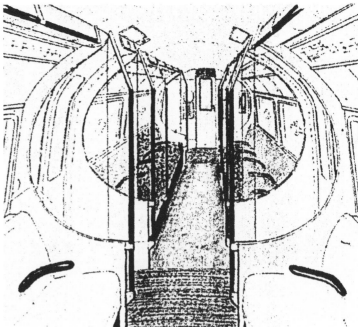

Above left Tilney Shane's initial design sketch exploring how extra illumination could be introduced into the car end areas.

Above Initial concept sketch

There were several key features of the existing cars which had not worn at all well in the 20 years since they were first built and which no longer met the enhanced travel expectations passengers held in the late 1980s. Top of the list was lighting. It will be recalled that the original solution was bare fluorescent tubes in ceiling recesses which had proven to cause considerable glare for both seated and standing passengers. In both car ends, there was no direct illumination at all which made these important areas rather murky and forbidding.

The original grey colour scheme was now looking very tired as was the original moquette pattern on the seating. Another feature which had proved to be an expensive maintenance item, as well as an eyesore, was the illuminated advertising. Half of these panels were typically out of action at any time and, lit or not, they displayed a dirty residue of tunnel dust. The individual spring loaded dangling handgrips were also a maintenance liability and there was a strong desire from the line to replace them with something better.

The car line diagrams were mounted on hinged panels which opened out for ventilation. This not only made them difficult to read in this position but also an accumulation of tunnel dust that had built up on the back over the years was presented to passengers at eye level.

Finally the existing armrest design was prone to breakage due to vandals walking on them!

Initial concept sketches were prepared which exploited a redesign of one of the main areas that had to be replaced due to the hazardous materials behind it; the ceiling. This provided the key to a new lighting concept where glass luminaires would now throw light over both a new ceiling profile and also illuminate with even brightness all of the passenger seating and standing areas of the car. Much-needed illumination was also introduced into the car end standing areas by the incorporation of round port hole lights.

A radical approach was chosen to reprofile the shape of the draughtscreens. These were given a curved form which then harmonised with the ceiling curve to produce an attractive ellipsoidal shape. This gave a more open and welcoming aspect to the entire car. The dangling handgrips were replaced by a series of vertical grab-poles which were mounted clear of the flooring to aid cleanability. Continuous horizontal handrails were also incorporated and much work was done to ensure that travellers of all sizes could readily find a convenient and comfortable handhold.

Armrests were redesigned and re-engineered. Their new profiled shape was more comfortable and pleasing and their structural integrity was much improved by solidly anchoring their concealed extension to an internal seat support structure. Most of the attractive original two-tier ones designed by DRU had by now been replaced by an unremarkable thin walled moulded plastic version.

Below left Most of the elements of the redesign are shown in this view such as curve of the draughtscreens forming an ellipse with the new ceiling profile, onto which light is cast by the form of new cast glass luminaires. The patterned blue panel adjacent to an advertisement was a design ploy to counter the unsightly appearance that was caused by unfilled advertisement panels. The ribbed handrail sections were initially keyed onto a steel rod but the flexing that occurred from cars in motion made this an untenable solution. They would soon be replaced by epoxy powder coated handrails and grabpoles.

Below right Close-up of the car end showing how effectively the light from the luminaires was cast onto the ceiling, also the port hole lights which brought much needed illumination into these areas.

Right The search to find a distinctive and memorable design for the seating moquette. The designers wished to re-interpret the bold and confident designs from the 1930s and '40s in a contemporary manner.

Far right The moquette design chosen for the 1967 Stock.

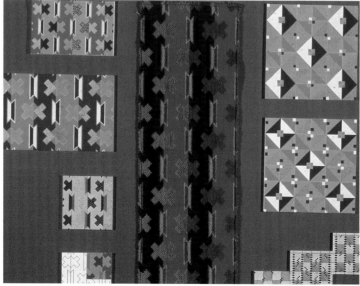

A standard production interior. This view shows the skilful integration of all of the individual elements (compare this to the original interior design of 1967 Stock) but the eagle eyed will see that the ventilation slots are now below the advertisements (before, they were directly under the luminaires). This was a change made to ease manufacture and assembly during the development process, but the downside has been that an unfortunate shadow is cast on top of the line diagrams.

A decision was made to retain the existing seating mix of longitudinal and transverse seats in both the driving motor and the trailer cars. This maintained the existing location of all operating equipment; however the seating was re-contoured to give the appearance of a more inviting, fuller upholstered seat and also to improve the seating ergonomics. Finally, ventilation panels, advertisement frames and car line diagram holders were all redesigned, giving an integrated appearance to all of these.

Colour was used in a bold, innovative way in order to make the interior more welcoming and reassuring. A warm ivory coloured powder coat was chosen for the interior panelwork, including the doors, and a 30 per cent gloss level was picked to reduce reflections and disguise minor surface imperfections. A blue shade related to the Victoria Line colour was used for the armrests, grab-poles and handrails, and experiments were made with a bold and confident moquette pattern (see visuals) to replace the dull and stale looking grey original design. Research was carried out in the LT Museum's archives to examine the classic pre- and post-war moquette designs by Marion Dorn, Paul Nash and Enid Marx, as the plan was to re-interpret their bold and innovative character in a manner appropriate to the 1990s.

Finally, the original ribbed maple wood flooring which had been a feature of London's underground trains since the beginning of the 20th century was replaced by a newly developed composite rubber material, finished in two tones of blue, the darker shade being used to delineate the door vestibules from the seating areas. This new coloured flooring played a major part in creating the completely new appearance, being much brighter and easier to clean than the wood's drab and dirty looking finish.

All of these ideas were developed into a partial full size mock-up and, following the approval of LT and LUL directors and senior managers, a decision was made in 1989 to gut completely two 4-car units and rebuild them as a prototype train in order to test the suitability of the design and its impact on the travelling public. It was also painted externally in one of the corporate liveries being evaluated at the time. It was soon decided that all of the refurbished trains would wear a painted livery in order to herald the significant changes that the public would see in the interior.

Market research was conducted in the autumn of 1989 on the prototype train and the results contained some of the most positive comments ever recorded regarding the design of London Underground's rolling stock.

There was a highly positive response to the new livery. Passengers felt that this displayed renewed operator pride in the rolling stock with the result that they

Above The cantilevered armrests and the grabpoles mounted clear of the floor to ease cleaning.

Below The first prototype train was painted in one of the liveries then being assessed (actually the horizontal blue window panel version), but shortly afterwards the livery shown here would be chosen for all train types. The proposal for the blue lower body panel came from one of London Underground's engineers, Mark Orsman.

themselves were also valued. Ninety per cent of the respondents said that they liked the new interior and considered it to be vastly superior in every way to the existing design dating from the mid-1960s. They readily identified with the fact that a successful coupling of colours and lighting, blended with the use of pleasing design features such as the port hole lights, were clearly created to provide an attractive, warm and welcoming environment for them, the passengers, rather than just being there to meet operational and engineering requirements.

In short, the passengers were delighted. They viewed this as a brand new train, not an extensively reworked 22 year old one, and considered that this was a very visible and successful manifestation of the way taxpayers' money was being spent by London Underground.

Perhaps the most important result achieved was the realisation that there is a strong relationship between the imagery of attractively designed rolling stock and the sense of personal security. Drab and ill-kempt rolling stock is associated with a threatening environment whereas the alternative is regarded not simply as more pleasant but as comparatively much safer.

Because of these remarkable research findings, the Victoria Line scheme was judged to be a winning formula, and its chief ingredients such as the ivory shell colour and the bold and confident moquette design, would be henceforth applied to all of the other refurbishment projects as well as the new-build Central, Jubilee and Northern Line trains.

Left The dedicated interior colour scheme for the Bakerloo trains which uses terracotta as the line reference colour on armrests and grabpoles. On the first production trains, ribbed plastic sections sleeved over a steel core were also used on grabpoles and handrails but these were later replaced by powder coated steel ones.

Below The moquette design used on these trains.

2. The 1972 Mark 2 Tube Stock Bakerloo Line trains

As we have seen, the close cousins of the 1967 Victoria Line trains were the 1972 Mark 2 Bakerloo Line trains and essentially the same interior design scheme was chosen for these as well, when their turn for refurbishment came at the end of 1991. Jones Garrard and Tilney Shane again developed the design concepts which this time featured the use of a terra-cotta colour as the line reference for grab-poles, arm-rests and a dedicated moquette design. These colour complemented the ivory interior scheme in a particularly successful manner and as a consequence, these trains are probably the best modern re-incarnation yet of all of the virtues (cosy, welcoming and inviting) of the much loved 1938 Stock.

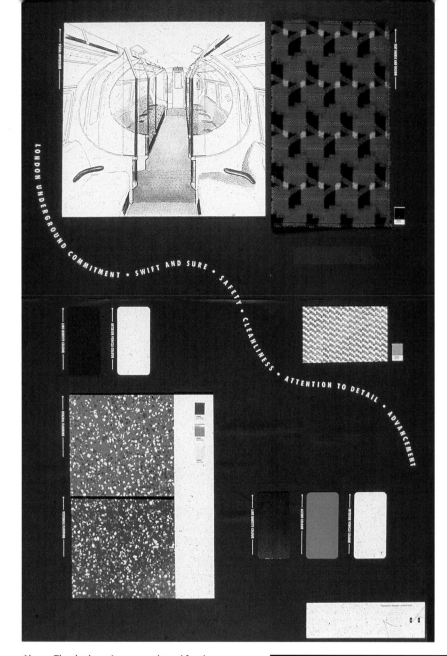

Above The designer's concept board for the Northern Line refurbishment.

Above right One of three trains that were converted into a Northern Line related interior with charcoal grey being used on grabpoles and armrests. Subsequently these would be changed into Bakerloo Line versions.

The *art deco* pattern chosen was also used in some of the Northern Line's 1959 Stock trains and, as shown here, some unrefurbished 1972 Mk1 Stock.

3. The 1972 Mark 1 Tube Stock Northern Line trains

Tilney Shane were, at the same time, also asked to develop a line related interior for the 1972 Mark 1 trains on the Northern Line and it was the original intention that these vehicles would also all be fully refurbished. As it happened, only three trains were completed because of budget constraints and the possibility of providing brand new leased trains for the Northern Line which was emerging as work on the three trains was in hand.

The designers' original concept board is illustrated, showing the development of their colour scheme and a moquette design with a deliberate art deco character. The intention was to evoke the style of the famous archer statue, created by Eric Aumonier at East Finchley station in 1939, which subsequently had been chosen as the line's symbol. The grabpoles were finished in charcoal grey since it was considered that black handrails and grabpoles would appear too hostile. In the event, neither colour would be acceptable to LT's Unit for Disabled Passengers. These three trains were put into service and the moquette design was also used in some of the line's fleet of 1959 Stock vehicles. One complete 1959 Stock train was also refurbished, the work including renewal of the maple wood flooring and the window pillar finishes. However, this was done on a like for like basis. This train was the only one of its generation to be painted (in the middle of 1993) in the final corporate livery and the end result was, surprisingly, very successful. Original fears that it might look like mutton dressed as lamb were totally unfounded!

4. The C69/77 Stock

The refurbishment of the C Surface Stock trains was the next phase in the programme and the improvements that the new passenger environment gained, both in terms of perceived safety and ambience, were probably even more impressive. The work was carried out from 1990 to 1994.

The vehicles had new car end windows which significantly enhanced perceptions of safety and security. The ivory interior shell colour of other refurbishments was retained and two tones of grey were chosen as accent colours. Finally these cars were fitted out with yellow grab-poles (as a reference to the Circle Line colour) and a new charcoal grey moquette design with colour references from the three lines on which these trains run. A ribbed composite rubber floor, similar to the previous refurbishments, was installed but this time it was in a medium grey colour loaded with ivory, yellow and dark grey coloured chips. Operating experience soon proved that this colour very successfully disguised soil and so it became the standard background colour for all other train types, but with other line-related colour chips added to it.

BREL were initially commissioned to examine various new features such as the elimination of the transverse bulkheads to give more open and welcoming interior space that would also enable alternative handrail solutions to be tried throughout the car. The original vehicles had also featured illuminated advertisements on these transverse bulkheads; these were equally unreliable and there was no wish to retain them. Two prototype vehicles were built incorporating a selection of different ideas and these entered service in November 1989 with market research findings guiding a final design specification.

A contract was then awarded to RFS Industries of Doncaster in 1990 to carry out refurbishment of the full fleet and at that stage Cre'Active Design Consultants were appointed to develop further the best of the ideas that had been demonstrated into a fully resolved design. They produced a full size mock-up of one third of an entire car to show these refinements. They were able to restore the full complement of 32 seats per car from the original trains by creating the longitudinal seats as pairs, separated by an armrest. Through full liaison and consultation with line representatives and LUL's design and engineering management teams, all the details from the mock-up were faithfully replicated within the production vehicles.

Notable features are the full depth glazed draughtscreens with their upper securing castings profiled for a comfortable grip, the moulded floor coving details which allowed for easy cleaning all around the car, and the close-coupled horizontal handrails. These give every passenger in these high capacity vehicles a convenient handhold in the greatly increased standing areas which this refurbishment programme created.

This photograph shows how the typical original interiors in tones of grey and pale blue laminate had become very dowdy and down at heel by the late 1980s. Not only that, but the visual residue of graffiti attack had also made these interiors appear hostile and intimidating. This was compounded by the walled-off transverse seats with high draughtscreens either side of the four sets of doors. These caused very poor through car visibility which had resulted in some unfortunate incidents concerning women passengers. Any redesign would need to address these safety issues as a matter of the greatest urgency.

Circle Line

Hammersmith & City Line

District Line

The modified prototype interiors built by BREL which entered passenger service in November 1989. Apart from changing all the hazardous materials, there was also an engineering requirement to reposition some of the underseat equipment. BREL (now Adtranz) at Derby were asked to examine these requirements by refitting a stripped out 2-car unit. The driving motor car was fully modified with all longitudinal seating, new grabpole and handrail postions, whereas the trailer car work was confined to revised poles and rails, material and colour changes.

Left The full size mock-up of one third of a car that was produced by Cre'Active shows a number of subtle differences from the production version below, but the design was substantially carried through to the refurbished trains.

Below This view of the chosen design readily demonstrates the security benefits that were achieved by the excellent through car visibility and the ease with which the interior of the following vehicle can be also observed via the newly specified car-end windows. The moquette pattern has references to three lines worked by these trains. The Hammersmith & City Line pink colour was not in existence when the pattern was designed.

During and after refurbishment. The picture taken at RFS's Doncaster Works shows how the cars were completely stripped back to a bare shell.

A refurbished C Stock train with its painted livery shown in the restored Gloucester Road Station.

5. The 1960/62 A Stock Metropolitan Line trains

The A60/62 Stock trains were similar in many respects to the Circle Line trains, since they presented the same tired, dreary and well-worn image, probably even more so since they were on average some 10 years older. The results of graffiti, both inside and out, had also made their appearance particularly threatening and hostile to passengers.

In 1989/90 Metro-Cammell were contracted to examine the refurbishment possibilities for this stock in two levels of work and DCA Design Consultants were appointed by the manufacturer to work with LUL on the project.

A 4-car unit was returned to LUL in June 1990 which demonstrated some major improvements, but it was not possible to incorporate the changes that would allow for the all important addition of car end windows until later on in the project.

As on the Circle Line trains the transverse bulkheads were removed in order to create a more airy and spacious interior, and the new smaller diameter fluorescent tubes which were now available were neatly integrated either side of a continuous ceiling panel structure. The original large solid fibreglass draughtscreens to the ceilings (which were particularly hazardous) were replaced by a new design featuring a neatly integrated and comfortably profiled grab handle. A bold new moquette design was developed in the same style as for the other train types and was also nicely accented by the now corporate ivory colour. A particularly successful feature was the continuous luggage rack with hand rails integrated. New hopper type windows were incorporated and finally a composite flooring solution was developed similar to that on the other train types.

Again this revised interior design was received extremely well, which was hardly surprising when it was compared with the existing design, but lack of funding prevented any further refurbishment going ahead in 1991. Indeed such was the

Concept visual produced by DCA in autumn 1989 showing their new draughtscreen design and the opened-out ceiling with integrated full length luggage racks.

Prior to DCA's involvement, motor car 5132 of A Stock was refitted in this style, employing individual seats with glass fibre backs. A more limited variant of this refit was applied to trailer car 6132.

Far left and left Two views of the interior of the 4-car unit built by Metro-Cammell which was returned to London Underground in June 1990. The open ceiling and the first proposed moquette design are two notable features.

Opposite page below The modified design for the entire fleet as built at ABB's Derby works from spring 1993 onwards.

Right The existing transverse ceiling bulkheads and luggage racks had to be retained for cost reasons. The concept of a line related feature colour was continued by the use of a rich magenta colour for grabpoles, handrails and handles.

financial situation that, at one stage, the remit was to preserve only the asset health of these vehicles; that is, to replace everything on a like for like basis.

However it was soon discovered by diligent project management, that an improved draught-screen of a new design could be purchased for the same price as the old one in new fire-safe material and so, little by little, the essentials of DCA's design concept were not only preserved but also, with their ongoing involvement, improved. ABB at Derby won the production contract to refurbish the fleet and the first car was completed in spring 1993. Although the final costings allowed the all important car end windows to be retained, it was unfortunately not possible to keep the continuous luggage racks and the opened out ceiling profile. The original luggage racks were cleaned and retained. However the redesign remains a very successful one with its safe, bright, warm welcoming interior that has a strong Metropolitan Line identity.

The significant improvements that had been made by the paints industry in anti-graffiti powder coated finishes were now to be incorporated in a 60 per cent gloss level for maximum effectiveness. This soon proved to be so successful that it has become LUL's standard prescribed finish, henceforth to be used on all future train types. This new interior, together with its painted corporate livery, has significantly extended the operating life of these trains, and in marketing terms, begins to bring them into contention with the competing mainline Chiltern Turbos which run parallel.

Below left Car end windows, an extremely important safety feature were added despite financial constraints.

Below Close up of the production moquette pattern.

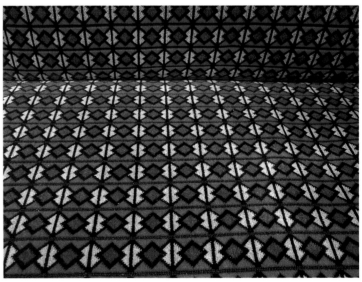

Right General interior view of one of the three cars converted at the end of 1990 by Metro-Cammell to designs prepared by the Transport Design Consortium. Car end windows were fitted and the two stainless steel luggage racks that were fitted for the Heathrow service are readily apparent.

Below Close up of one of the racks featuring a notional seat. The circular hooped handrail that was fitted to one of the cars can be seen in this view.

6. The 1973 Tube Stock Piccadilly Line trains

Although the first train of the refurbished 1973 Stock was officially launched in May 1996, the history of the project goes back to the middle of 1990. The Transport Design Consortium was then asked to develop proposals for an extensive modernisation of these trains with Messrs Tilney, Lumsden & Shane again leading the interior design work. As with all the other trains, the original interior design was now looking extremely faded and tired; furthermore there were many awkward and crudely detailed components as well as unco-ordinated and unintegrated features within it which now looked extremely dated. These gave considerable scope to improve every aspect of the train's interior in order to bring it into line with the standards now established for the other lines. However, what was really required (since the current arrangement was clearly inadequate) was the provision of generous spaces to house passengers' luggage travelling to and from Heathrow.

TLS started to examine alternative concepts for the central area of these cars by analysing various seating arrangements including cross seats of reduced width which would ensure that travellers could have sight of, and be able to touch, their luggage.

Car end windows, deep glazed draughtscreens, a similar grab-pole and handrail treatment to the 1967/72 Stocks were also developed, as were bright new moquette and flooring designs. Two folding stainless steel luggage racks per car were proposed in the central sections and additional tip up seats were also suggested to make up for the normal seating that had been lost.

A 3-car unit was converted at the end of 1990 which remained in passenger service until 1995. A market research study was undertaken to examine not just the impact of the new decor and the car end windows, but specifically the slightly different variants of luggage rack (one with its own seat cushion), and the different combinations of seating in the centre of each car.

The results were that respondents were very positive about the interiors stating significantly that "... the new cars are orientated to people rather than solely to transport. The carriages seem a lot more roomy and cheerful with good utilisation of space". The redesigned luggage areas elicited strong likes and dislikes. They were considered to be marvellous for the Heathrow service but an imposition for the Rayners Lane branch of the line and for the central London commuter.

Warwick Design's original mock-up of their proposal for the refurbishment of the 1983 Jubilee Line trains. London Underground's original intention was to modernise the existing fleet with this design and then order a further batch of vehicles to accommodate the line's extension. In the event, elements of the work were used on the 1973 Stock refurbishment.

Warwick Design's first mock-up for 1973 Stock with car end windows, perch seating and the luminaire line continuing in an uninterrupted manner from one car end, over the doors to the other end; in the manner of the original 1983s. To meet the demands for better passenger information which arose out of the research findings, passenger information displays and vastly improved passenger audio information were added to the specification. The scope of work was extended to include major modifications to the cab, to improve the train operator's comfort and convenience.

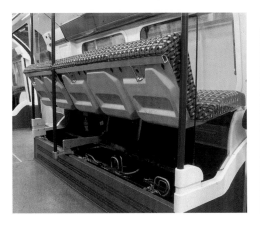

Far left Not only is the interior of refurbished 1973 Stock a vast improvement on the original but it was also skilfully re-designed to facilitate maintenance requirements.

Left The extra deep standback area for cases and buggies etc. The moquette trimmed perch seats align nicely with the seat tops.

Above Detail of an early production interior of refurbished 1973 Stock photographed at the Bombardier plant at Wakefield.

Above right Bank of seats showing the moquette design.

Below Two of the pleasing sculptural details of the redesign. The single piece horizontal handrail rises to obtain the correct head clearance over the double doors.

Unfortunately the provision of dedicated trains with these features for the Heathrow service, which originally had been considered, was now operationally not possible and so a more flexible universal solution was sought by the business.

Warwick Design Consultants had just finished the design work for a major refurbishment of the Jubilee Line 1983 Stock and had produced a full size mock-up. The original plan was that extensively refurbished stock to this design, together with a further batch of new trains built in the same style, was to serve the extended line. However, following a decision made by the Jubilee Line Extension's Project Team that an entire fleet of all-new trains would instead be ordered for the line, it was suggested their design could be adapted to meet the Piccadilly Line's requirements. This was particularly attractive to the development team since the trains of 1983 Stock were closely related to 1973 Stock.

What was of significant interest was the fact that very large multi-purpose extended standbacks which increased standing capacity by 20 per cent were a key part of this design (these had been designed to accommodate a wheelchair, a major part of the design brief since the new stations on the extension would be fully accessible to people in wheelchairs).

The decision was then taken to award the design contract to Warwick Design for the Piccadilly Line trains and give the refurbishment work to RFS Industries Limited.

Unfortunately half way through the development stage, RFS Industries Limited went into receivership and, after a protracted period which was fraught with problems, their passenger rail business was sold to Bombardier Transportation Limited in spring 1994 who subsequently inherited the contract.

The previous interior design had been closely developed to accord with the contractor's specific skills and production working methods; however the engineers and technicians at BTL started to redevelop many areas of the car their way. It was soon obvious that the integrity of the original design was being heavily compromised and so a new management team, involving Warwick Design, Bombardier Prorail, London Underground engineers, project managers and the writer, developed a new mock-up which was then signed off by all parties.

One of six dot matrix train destination displays within each car.

Below A novel method of presenting information for passengers from King's Cross to Hammersmith has been integrated into the panelwork above the perch seats in the deep standback areas; this presents tourist information about places of interest along the Piccadilly Line's route. The cheerful and friendly style of this information is fully in keeping with the bright, warm and welcoming character of these 'new' trains.

This management process was a complete success because the production vehicles are extremely faithful to the revised mock-up as the illustrations show. Details such as the new fan housings, handrail catenary castings, luminaires and the skilful integration of CCTV cameras have been particularly well interpreted. The trains were rebuilt at typically one third of the cost of new ones.

Finally an extremely ingenious and effective folding cab door has been designed for these trains by Jones-Garrard. This provides rapid, reliable and convenient emergency detrainment to augment all of the enhanced safety features now built into these trains. The external painted corporate livery suits the proportions of this train particularly well; line identity graphics and a smart modification to the windows to mask the extended standbacks all complement its sleek external appearance. Perhaps their greatest success is the manner in which they now continue the quality ambience of air travel from the aircraft, through the terminal buildings and the Underground's platforms to give the appropriate gateway experience right into central London.

Below left The folding emergency detrainment steps, designed by Jones-Garrard Limited.

Below The neat exterior applied graphic treatment which obscures the new interior panelling required to create the deeper multi-purpose standback spaces.

One of the initial refit proposals from 1996.

7. The 1978 Stock District Line trains

This was the last train type of the fleet to be refurbished and unlike all of the other work programmes the gestation period to develop a suitable design solution was an extremely long one, four years in fact! Jones-Garrard were originally appointed back in the middle of 1996 to produce initial concepts for a redesigned interior but a prototype vehicle was not finally completed until September 2000. There have been many reasons for this lengthy development period, not least the fact that the fire safety performance of the existing interior was still very good and therefore there had not been the same pressure for change as there had been with all of the other train designs. The original design was also going to be a 'harder act to follow' than the others for in its day it had been a particularly accomplished solution.

The vehicles built by Metro-Cammell for the Hong Kong Mass Transit system during the same period as D Stock had featured a fully open inter-car connection from new, and it was natural that the designers of the D Stock refit would recommend a similar approach in their earliest concepts, as the spacious 'square-rigged' bodies would benefit tremendously from such a proposition. Unfortunately the major costs involved soon ruled this out from the scope of work but car end windows would still promote perceptions of greater safety and security by opening up the car end spaces.

In the natural manner of the design development process, the concepts were then reviewed internally and the results fed back to the design consultants, after which a Stage 2 report document was prepared at the beginning of 1997. This time around, the ideas illustrated were market researched and both engineering and maintenance staff were given every opportunity to input their own views on important issues such as maintenance and cleaning.

A final Stage 3 report was produced in March 1998 by Jones-Garrard which was their response to and interpretation of all of the areas that they had been asked to address. The illustrations confirmed all of the decisions made and took the form of very impressive, highly convincing CAD visuals. Some of these are reproduced on this spread.

General view of the saloon with curved grabpoles, passenger information modules and the final ceiling profile with edge lighting.

Car end detail showing windows and multi-purpose area with two tip-up seats.

A longitudinal seating bay with the final design of armrest and draughtscreens.

The vestibule showing passenger alarm, door buttons and the priority seats.

DOUBLE HEIGHT COLOUR SPLIT DESIGNATES ZONE

Both cantilevered and looped armrests were explored (with the Line preferring the latter type for reasons of strength) and an early concept sketch includes the two-piece treatment that would end up in the prototype.

Above In the spring of 1999 London Underground asked Cre'Active Design Consultants to 'engineer' the final interior design with a brief to maintain the overall concept of Jones-Garrard's work as closely as possible. Cre'Active have engineered a very strong yet elegant ceiling profile with adequate box sections housed within its structure. It has to contain four tangential fan units (two in the middle of the car and one at each end which blow cool air towards both longitudinal seating bays in turn). Lighting is achieved by curved opalescent glass shrouds which effectively illuminate the total ceiling area.

Left Part of the door vestibule area showing the articulated low level handrail (reminiscent of the one used on classic RT and RM buses) which Cre'Active developed to maximise convenience in entry particularly from those platforms which are not level with the car floor.

The highly successful refurbishment of all the trains reviewed in this chapter has proved beyond doubt that the way forward for future train designs is that their body structures will be engineered on the basis that an existing interior can be 'thrown away' at the half-way period of a typical 30–40 year lifespan. It can then be replaced by a brand-new one that can fully exploit all of the up-to-the-minute technological advances and design concepts available. Today's passengers have very high expectations and they do not want to travel in outdated trains. Refurbishment is a successful formula that can keep vehicles up to date in a cost-effective manner.

CHAPTER NINE

New Jubilee and Northern trains

Jubilee Line

For the design history of these trains we must go back to the spring of 1991 when it was the original intention to provide sufficient trains for the extended Jubilee Line by totally refurbishing the existing fleet of 1983 Stock and then ordering a further batch of brand new vehicles to this extensively revised design for the expanded service. Warwick Design Consultants were appointed to carry out this work and shown below are their first interior renderings and concept boards as shown to management; these led to the manufacture of a fully finished half car mock-up which was completed in their premises by July 1991. The intention was to express the royal connotations of the Silver Jubilee which had inspired the line's name by exploiting a rich silvery look with accents of purple and aquamarine.

The interior design also featured quadrant shaped tip-up seats at the car ends and two continuous bands of glass luminaires running between car ends to create the appearance of a continuous edge-lit ceiling. The appearance problem of the previous ugly ceiling fan castings was effectively tackled by housing the fans within a soft elliptical shape formed in the ceiling panel. Part of Warwick Design's remit was also to upgrade the cab design of the 1983 Stock with respect to the incorporation of updated features and improved ergonomics, and they built a full size study model which is illustrated opposite.

A period of intensive political activity then followed. The Jubilee Line Extension was given Royal Assent in March 1992 but a £400 million contribution from the developers of Canary Wharf was part of the financial package that would enable the Bill to proceed. Just as it emerged from Parliament in 1992, the Canary Wharf developers went into receivership. However by October 1993 financial restructuring had been completed and the JLE was finally on its way.

Throughout this uncertain period, a dedicated Jubilee Line project team had been

Below Warwick Design's original concept visual for the major refurbishment of 1983 Stock.

Below right Concept board showing early alternatives for a dedicated seat moquette design.

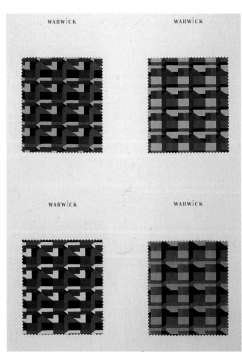

retained by the Government and part of their work was to reassess the overall design and manufacturing approach for the trains. They concluded after careful analysis that a fleet of brand new trains could be purchased for virtually the same cost as the original proposal to refurbish the existing stock extensively and then buy more of the same. This was really not surprising in the light of the great strides that had been made over the previous decade in building car bodies from welded aluminium extrusions. The Central Line vehicles and the various Networker trains for British Rail had already pointed the way ahead.

As a result of this a contract was awarded at the end of 1993 to GEC Alsthom Metro-Cammell Limited to design and build 59 new 6-car passenger trains, each vehicle being 17.8 metres in length. These would be of welded aluminium extrusion construction, and like the Central Line trains would feature externally hung doors. To support their initial bid to the Jubilee Line Extension's team, MCL asked Trevor Scott Associates (designers of the British Rail Networker trains) to prepare various options for an all new cab design at the beginning of 1992 and these are illustrated. With regard to the interior design, it was decided that, rather than start all over again, Warwick Design's existing solution could be effectively transferred into these new cars with additional development to meet the client team's requirements and the

Above left Full size mock-up built by Warwick Design Consultants in mid 1991 showing their proposal for a major refurbishment of 1983 Stock. Clearly visible are:
• the brushed stainless steel facings of the single leafed doors, the original stainless steel grabpoles with purple accents and the aquamarine feature colour designed to promote a *Royal Silver Jubilee* connotation to reflect the origin of the line name;
• the quadrant shaped tip-up seats at the car end and the continuous bank of cast glass luminaires;
• the tip-up seats within the large standback area to accommodate a wheelchair;
• the softly profiled fan castings which would eventually re-appear on refurbished 1973 Stock.

Above Mock-up of the cab redesigned by Warwick Design showing two platform monitors positioned over the cab access door.

The design that was produced by Trevor Scott Associates at the beginning of 1992 to support Metro-Cammell's initial bid. The symbols in the small circular window were to indicate the two functions required to both open the door for normal access and also to actuate it for its folding detrainment ramp mode. This was known as the flush door cab option.

adaptations required by the monocoque structure. It was a natural development of this decision to then appoint Warwick Design to also work on both the interior and exterior of the cab, as well as the design of its integrated emergency detrainment system. The contract was placed with MCL, but since it was written around a previously agreed interior design specification the result was that some design constraints, such as keeping the same window proportions as the coachbuilt 1983 Stock, were imposed. It is for this reason that the large panoramic windows that were developed for the 1992 Central Line trains were not specified.

However, these car bodies, built and painted by a member company of the Alsthom group in Barcelona, nevertheless feature a different and very neatly executed detail in which all of the passenger windows are ribbon glazed, i.e. each set of two passenger window panels is visually integrated by black painted accents to create the impression of sleek, continuous window panelling. The cab is again different from that of the 1992 Stock in that the front facing 'M' door incorporates folding detrainment steps which are speedily and simply deployed by operating a handle and pushing open, gravity and gas struts then providing a controlled opening. As mentioned above, Warwick Design did the engineering design and prototyping work for these detrainment steps and a contract was then awarded to Westinghouse for their further development into production. This is the reason for the relatively small centre cab window; the rest of the door space is required to house the folded steps.

This fact also explains why both of the cab windows either side are angled in order to have a visual relationship with the centre one and the individual charcoal grey mask of the livery is again used to integrate the cab grab handles. Flat missile proof glass is once again used since crash pillars are located at the corners of the cab and adjacent to its detrainment door. These provide the highest level of crashworthiness yet achieved by any design of tube train; the car is able to withstand a 100 tonnes end load without deformation of the body structure. Had the stylish wrap-around cab

Above Four alternative treatments of cab design that were also explored by Trevor Scott. In each design the two specific cab door opening functions are clearly distinguishable. The smaller asymmetrically positioned cab door window certainly broke new ground in giving a novel face to a London tube train. The version on the bottom right with its traditional size of cab door window immediately recalls the appearance of 1983 Stock.

Right Work in progress at Warwick Design.

Early visual from Warwick Design examining how the cab door with its folded steps could be satisfactorily integrated within the overall cab styling.

windows of 1973 Stock been perpetuated, their corners would even so have been filled in by these pillars, as was the case on BR's Class 442 Wessex Electrics designed by Jones-Garrard. The high-intensity headlamps, light emitting diode tail lights and detrainment lights are surrounded by an elliptical mask which adds a pleasing element of form to the cab face.

As far as the interior design is concerned, Warwick Design were commissioned by GEC in February 1994 to build a new saloon mock-up to GEC's engineering drawings which were their own interpretation of the design consultancy's original scheme! This somewhat untenable state of affairs was resolved when Warwick were appointed by the JLE's own Rolling Stock project team to work with GEC on their behalf to address and resolve the design issues that were being highlighted as part of the normal development process. This ensured that the interior, the cab layout and ergonomics together with the cab's exterior styling would all receive the necessary attention.

Since the stations on the Jubilee Line Extension are the first on the network to be designed with proper wheelchair entry and exit points, each car has designated areas where up to four wheelchair passengers can be safely and securely accommodated. A low level handrail is provided to help them orientate themselves into the correct position which is either facing the direction of travel or at 180 degrees to it. Perch seats

Below left Scale model built by Warwick Design showing their cab design with emergency detrainment steps deployed.

Below right The same model with steps stowed behind the door. It shows the overall cab styling as finally agreed.

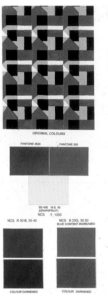

are fitted to these spaces so that they can be used when not required for wheelchairs or mothers with buggies. The handrail colour was originally of natural stainless steel finish because this continued the line relationship theme which had started with the refurbished Victoria and the new build Central Line trains. Lightly brushed stainless steel is however the worst of all finishes for the visually impaired and so they were changed to a pale yellow colour – grapefruit – a recommendation made by the Institute of Consumer Ergonomics of Loughborough.

The original feature colours of aquamarine and purple were nevertheless retained but the moquette pattern received a trace of yellow so that it was in harmony with the rest of the colour scheme. Great care was taken to ensure that there would be adequate horizontal handholds available for crush loaded passengers who found themselves standing in the multi-purpose areas. As far as has been practicable the ceiling has been slightly profiled to optimise headroom and to ensure that light is thrown onto it from the continuous bank of luminaires, thus ensuring a very even and bright light-spread throughout the entire length of each car. Real time passenger information modules are located between the line diagrams and the framed advertisements.

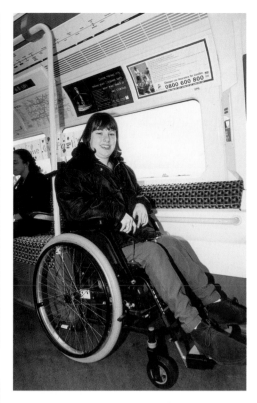

Opposite page:

Top The production version in service showing the flush ribbon-glazed passenger windows.

Centre left Revised concept board showing how yellow was introduced into the seat pattern design.

Below right The final mock-up built by Warwick Design at the GEC Metro-Cammell Washwood Heath plant. The previous brushed stainless steel handrails and grabpoles are replaced by pale yellow ones to meet the visibility needs of the partially sighted.

Bottom The production moquette pattern.

This page:

Top One of the four multi-purpose areas per car which safely accommodates a wheelchair.

Top right A young lady in her wheelchair safely tucked into her designated space. The low level hand rail below the perch seat is at its correct ergonomic height for positioning and she also has a low level passenger alarm handle within easy reach. Passenger door controls are also set at this same height within the door covings throughout the car.

Above Close-up detail of one of the passenger information modules, of which there are four per car.

Left View of three production Jubilee Line trains taken inside the impressive Stratford Market Depot. Neatly incorporated within elliptical surrounds each side of the front of the trains are the high intensity headlamps, light emitting diode tail lamps and detrainment lights.

Aerospace technology meets London Underground! The computer generated view through the cab window of a training simulator can accurately replicate the complete length of the Jubilee Line.

The cab interior was designed by Warwick using established ergonomic criteria in respect of all driving functions. The cab console incorporates two liquid crystal monitors which display pictures of station platforms. A third screen located on the offside wall forms part of the train management system. Air conditioning is provided to improve the driver's environment and the trains are equipped for manual or fully automatic operation. A training simulator was also developed which, in the manner of aircraft flight simulators, provides the trainee driver with a fully finished cab environment which is indistinguishable from the real product. A computer generated travelling view of any part of the complete line can be provided through the cab windows.

The first production train of what would be known as 1996 Stock entered service on the Jubilee Line on Christmas Eve 1997 with subsequent trains being progressively brought into service from January 1998 onwards. All of the 1983 Mark 1 Stock vehicles were then rapidly replaced with the final train of that type running on the Line on the 9th July 1998.

The visuals that were prepared by DCA Design Consultants to support Bombardier Transportation's tender for new Northern Line trains in 1993. They show the external cab styling and the interior view of the passenger saloon with curved grabpoles making their first appearance in a design offering for London Underground.

Northern Line

During 1993, ABB, GEC-Alsthom Metro-Cammell and Bombardier Transportation each took part in a competitive bidding programme to tender for brand new rolling stock for the Northern Line. Predictably the offerings from the first two companies were heavily based on their existing current tube train designs but Bombardier Transportation commissioned DCA Design Consultants to prepare brand new concepts to support their bid. These proposals show a cab styling treatment, cab interior design and a saloon interior with curved grabpoles making a first appearance.

In the end GEC-Alsthom Metro-Cammell won with a train design which was in appearance terms virtually identical to that of the Jubilee Line except that externally the cab door would now have a deeper window (because a different design of folding detrainment steps designed by Jones-Garrard would now be fitted). This had the effect of improving the cab's external appearance because the angled cab windows aligned more successfully with it. Two-thirds of the major components would come from

Right Early visual by Warwick Design to meet the Northern Line management team's request for a dedicated interior identity. Armrests and passenger information modules were finished in the uncompromising line colour – black! Even the left hand door pillars are black, though optional dark grey appears on the right side.

Below Concept board illustrating early thoughts for a dedicated moquette pattern and, below it, the production design.

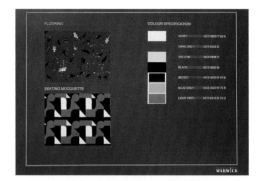

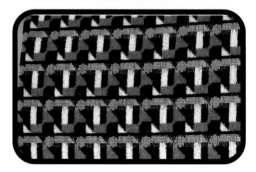

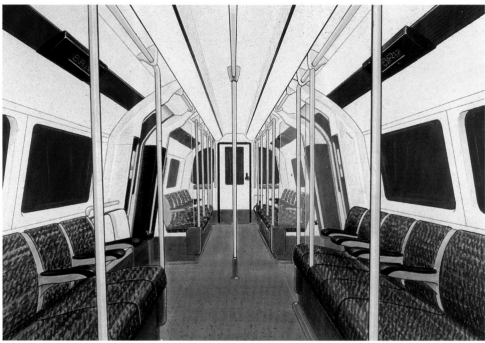

different sources. For example, they would have Adtranz bogies built in Derby, rather than the French GEC-Alsthom product used on the Jubilee trains, and although traction equipment and bodyshells are from the same suppliers, they are not identical. Furthermore air suspension is specified. The Northern Line started to receive the first of these brand new fleet of 106 trains from late 1998 onwards.

The only way that the line could get these urgently required trains was via a service provision package worth £40-45 million a year. Under the terms of this leasing deal, GEC-Alsthom (now Alstom Transport Limited) supply the trains under a Private Finance Initiative, and as well as running the line's maintenance depots, are also responsible for providing trains for service each day over a 20 year period. This PFI means that the entire cost of the trains was arranged by GEC-Alsthom using an operating lease – two major banks purchased the trains for London Underground. These will be leased back over an agreed timescale, thus offering funding and cashflow benefits. Alstom will continue to maintain an interest in the trains and they take the residual value risk. A product upgrade option is also written in to avoid technical obsolescence and Alstom and London Underground will therefore work together to add future technological developments and features to the trains and also improve their performance.

The interior design of the cars has been given a dedicated Northern Line identity by Warwick Design, with its own moquette, flooring pattern and accents such as the armrest mouldings and real time information surrounds finished in black; ventilation grilles are finished in a complementary satin silver finish. This is a response to the desire to create a dedicated Northern Line look which was a particular requirement of the line's management team. Tip-up seats replace the perch seating of the Jubilee Line variant in the multi-purpose areas. Both of these train types are now set to serve Londoners until typically the year 2033, albeit with probably at least one extensive interior refit during their lifetimes.

New Northern Line trains in service. Note the deeper centre cab window panel which, unlike the Jubilee Line version, aligns with the change of angle of the cab window, thus giving a more satisfactory appearance.

Below General view of the interior with the armrests and passenger information modules changed to black and the ventilation grilles now in satin silver. Tip-down seats are fitted in the multi-purpose area.

CHAPTER TEN

Space train and Accessible train

Below Simplified views comparing the Space train's cross-section with that of 1967 Tube Stock. The significant contribution made by smaller diameter wheels to the overall design is readily apparent.

Below right One-sixth scale models comparing the interior of Space train with that of the 1996 Tube Stock. They show how the revolutionary concept of the former is such a remarkable leap forward over its evolutionary equivalent, which had not significantly changed from the earliest days of tube railways!

Underground trains have changed considerably in recent years as they have harnessed the benefits gained by dramatic technological advances. The high expectations of a passenger generation which has grown up used to the convenience of personal transport have also helped shape these changes and as a consequence, all trains will probably continue to undergo a major rebuild at half life in order to capitalise on the latest developments and ideas.

The 'Space train' design concepts represent a radical clean sheet of paper approach to the design of new tube trains for London and as such contains some remarkably fresh and original thinking. The inspiration for the work started back in 1994 when John Vint, then Chief Rolling Stock Engineer for London Underground, initially asked

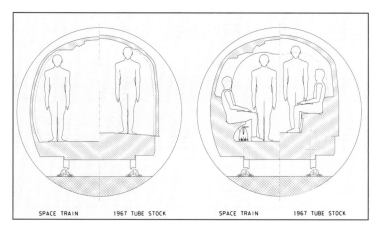

Above One sixth scale model showing the car exterior with doors open. The purpose of the yellow upswept perforated panels is to enable illumination of the platform/train interface from a train mounted light source. A model of a complete train can be seen alongside.

Above right Close-up view of the suggested treatment of the articulation point straddling a four wheel bogie of completely new design.

Chris Sharp, Senior Design Engineer, to examine other methods of collecting a train's operating current by replacing the time honoured method of current collection via live third and fourth rails. This request has been prompted by the high incidence of collector shoe breakages whose costly replacements had been causing him great concern. A roof mounted collector running on a positive rail, with negative return through the running rails (a conventional system used on other Metros) had a lot to commend it and the incorporation of this new feature became the springboard for a completely new design proposition. Other key features which had been on the wish list for many years were level, stepless access between platform and car floor, articulation, smaller wheels, a larger internal space envelope and wide inter-car access. These were also

incorporated, with the result that an increase in passenger capacity from around 40 per cent to 46 per cent in crush loaded conditions became a possibility when compared with conventional tube train design.

All of the extremely impressive and original design work described and illustrated in this final chapter has been developed by Chris Sharp and his assistant, Andrew Dean. The fact that the 1967 Victoria Line stock would be the next tube train type due for renewal provided the initial focus for the design activity, but the proposals could thereafter be equally applied to other tube lines. Other decisive factors were the realities that the whole route is in tunnel with straight station platforms throughout and there is no interworking with other routes (as occurs on the Piccadilly, Bakerloo and Jubilee Lines) to add complications.

A simplified cross sectional view compares the existing 1967 Stock with the Space train envelope whose near-circular cross section, lower floor and smaller wheels

Computer generated perspective view showing Space train docked at a platform with the collector extended to its operating position.

Below left Engineering layout drawing of a lateral section illustrating the amount of space available for standing and seated passengers. The floor height of conventional tube stock is shown by a chain dotted line.

Below How Space train's larger body section compares with that of 1996 Stock (proposed to be 218 mm wider at its broadest point).

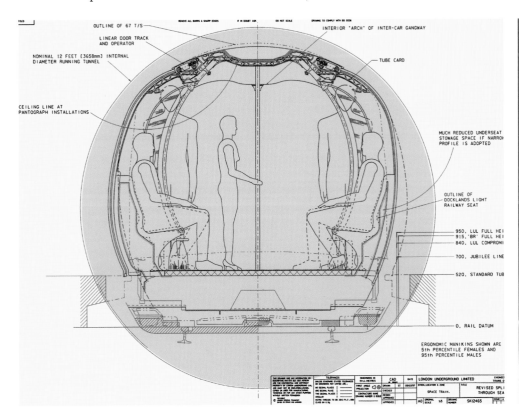

Facing page top A perspective view prepared by APA Design of Derby shows Space train centrally berthed in a platform with both platform screens and train doors open. A profiled front end is suggested and, *inset at base of page,* a notional design of detrainment ramp is shown deployed. With fully automatic operation and these screens, it is only necessary for the 22 double doors, each opening to a clear width of 1500 mm, to be inside the 132.5 mm distance between the relay rooms at each end of the Victoria Line's platforms.

Facing page bottom View with doors closed and platform screens removed showing the overhead power pick-up rail.

Above left Interior view of the one-sixth scale model demonstrating the exceptional potential for spacious passenger accommodation.

Above right Different view of the same interior study model at the point of articulation.

dramatically show how the greatly increased passenger space has been achieved. Even more impressive are the two sectioned scale models that compare Space train with 1996 Stock. Key dimensions that enable these tremendous advances in usable passenger space and convenience to be achieved are:

— At 3078 mm, the Space train is an impressive 218 mm wider each side at waist level than existing tube stock.

— The floor is 156mm lower than 1967 Stock at the car centre-line and 139 mm at the doorway sill plate in the tare condition. This gives level access by wheelchairs and buggies etc from London Underground's 520 mm high tube platforms with a 75 mm gap as currently stipulated within the 1997 Disability Discrimination Act (some alteration to platform edges would be necessary before the trains could operate).

— Each train would typically be made up from 11 articulated cars (although 10 to 13 cars have been evaluated within the overall length fixed by platforms) which are mounted on 13 bogies. Twenty-two sets of double doors would be fitted at 5886 mm intervals per car body and 6216 mm from car to car. Platform edge screen doors are also part of the design concept.

— The aisle width between longitudinal seats created by the new car body cross-section is 1512 mm which compares with 981 mm on existing stock types. This provides a significant increase in floor area of 49.5 per cent; a major gain for standing passengers. In fact the comparative dimensions for crush loading in the aisles and the vestibule areas are even more impressive – a 43.7 per cent increase in the room available for standing passengers between the aisles and a 63 per cent increase created by the much larger vestibules. These spaces are supplemented by the large area of the rotating turntable at the point of articulation which, with its narrow draughtscreens also provides exceptional through car mobility. The minimum width of 1680 mm at this significant point compares with an inter-car door width of only 650 mm on contemporary tube and surface stock trains (which passengers are only allowed to use in an emergency). Such a dimension would encourage easier and more convenient distribution of passengers throughout a crowded train.

— While much of the increase in floor area is due to the extra car width, seated passengers are set back to exploit the near circular cross-section of Space train. There are 290 seats available per train compared to the 304 in 1967 Stock which is a 4.6 per

View into the door vestibule showing an earlier treatment of the seating adjacent to the draughtscreen.

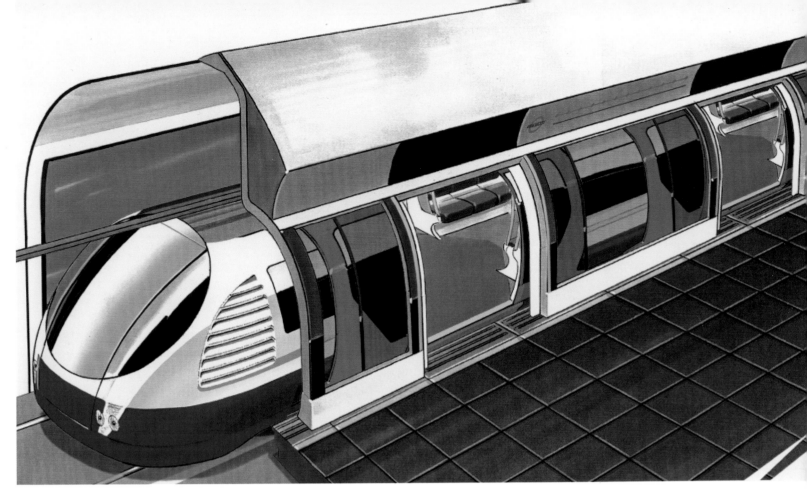
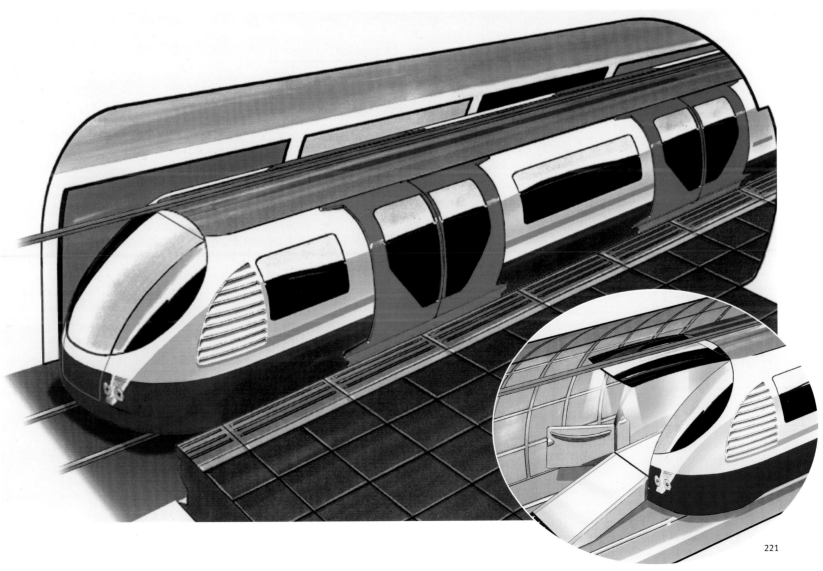

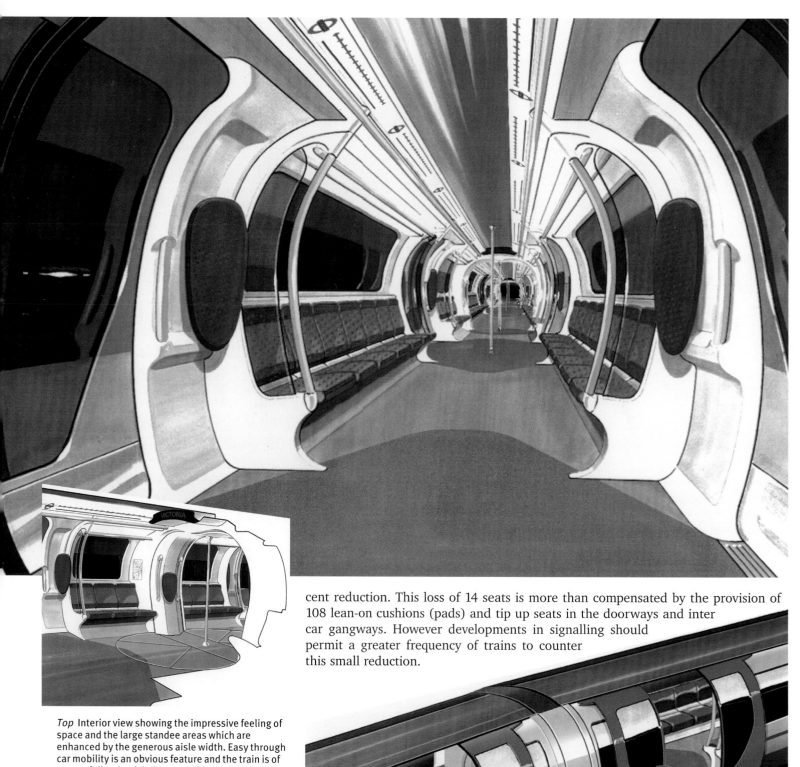

cent reduction. This loss of 14 seats is more than compensated by the provision of 108 lean-on cushions (pads) and tip up seats in the doorways and inter car gangways. However developments in signalling should permit a greater frequency of trains to counter this small reduction.

Top Interior view showing the impressive feeling of space and the large standee areas which are enhanced by the generous aisle width. Easy through car mobility is an obvious feature and the train is of course fully wheelchair compatible; at designated wheelchair positions, two standard seat modules would be replaced by two tip-seats to enable the required space to be created. The interior features hidden light sources which are projected onto the ceiling and the leaning pads for passengers in enlarged standbacks (when compared to conventional tube stocks) are another innovative feature. They are designed to ensure that the full door throughway width is available for as high a percentage of traffic hours as is possible.

Above Interior view at the point of articulation with the plan of the turntable geometry shown in its latest form. The leaning pads are repeated at this position.

Right Exterior view of the articulation point in its evolved form illustrating the close fit of the train to the platform edge and level access.

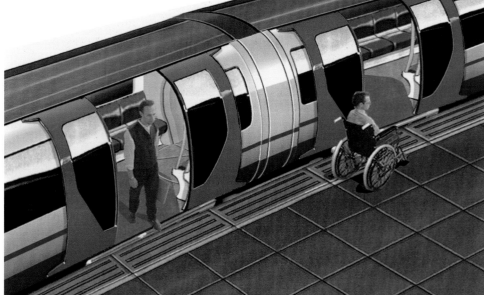

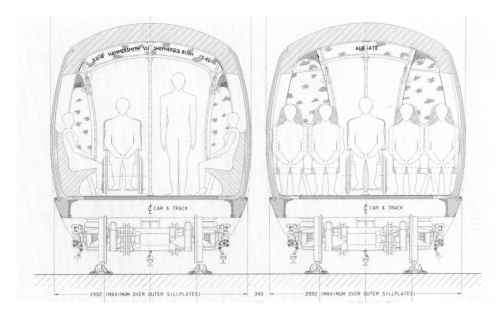

The cross-sectioned views showing proposals for both longitudinal and transverse seating at different points within a car. Passing clearances are also indicated.

Sub-surface variant – the Accessible train

Concept designs for a sub-surface big-brother variant of Space train have also been developed by Chris Sharp and his team. A variety of different train lengths and seating layouts have been investigated so that one basic vehicle design could ultimately be used on all of the sub-surface lines, with variation in door positions and internal layout to suit the different requirements. As this concept would require much less alteration to the infrastructure, it is probably more likely to be realised in the near future than its tube counterpart.

The outstanding passenger oriented design features will dramatically improve travel comfort and convenience. Just as on Space train, the Accessible train promises remarkable spaciousness with through gangways and articulated connections between cars. The distinctive personality of the interior treatments, where innovative lighting and colour accents play such an important role, recalls the very best of the fresh and inviting designs on main line services such as Heathrow Express.

As the Underground entered the 21st Century, it was being reorganised to engage in public-private partnerships to finance its future needs. Among the questions raised by this was whether the new partnerships would seize the nettle to underwrite the substantial engineering and technical challenges that must be overcome to preserve the integrity of these adventurous and ground-breaking concepts. Only time will tell.

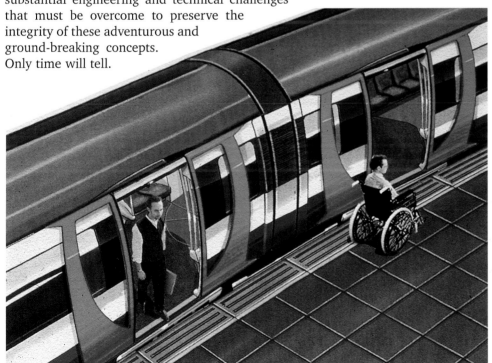

The articulation between cars of the Accessible train, again showing the level access feature.

Above left The interior view at the articulation point showing a car with longitudinal seating fitted throughout which would be suitable for the Circle and Hammersmith & City lines. Note the downlighters over the leaning pads. The real-time passenger information displays are shown neatly integrated with part of the roof support structure.

Above Another variant with a mix of transverse and longitudinal seats (Metropolitan or District lines).

Left The exceptionally open and spacious articulation area between the two cars.

Right Our final view shows the destination display module at the top of the doorway area, the ideal position for passengers to confirm the destination before they board. A line diagram is positioned on the back of this display as can be seen in the illustration above.